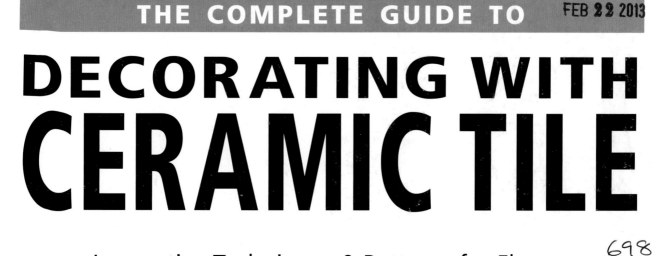

BLACK&DECKER

THE COMPLETE GUIDE TO

DECORATING WITH CERAMIC TILE

Innovative Techniques & Patterns for Floors,
Walls, Backsplashes & Accents

by Jerri Farris

Creative Publishing
international

MINNEAPOLIS, MINNESOTA
www.creativepub.com

Creative Publishing international

Copyright © 2007
Creative Publishing international, Inc.
400 First Avenue North, Suite 300
Minneapolis, Minnesota 55401
1-800-328-3895
www.creativepub.com

Printed at R.R. Donnelley

10 9 8 7 6 5 4 3

Library of Congress Cataloging-in-Publication Data

Farris, Jerri.
  The Complete guide to decorating with ceramic tile : innovative techniques & patterns for floors, walls, backspashes & accents / by Jerri Farris.
      p. cm.
  At head of title: Branded by Black & Decker.
  Summary: "Includes all of the basics and traditional techniques as well as new projects for walls, floors, bathrooms, kitchens, and the outdoors"--Provided by publisher.
  Includes index.
  ISBN-13: 978-1-58923-333-1 (soft cover)
  ISBN-10: 1-58923-333-6 (soft cover)
  1. Tile laying--Amateurs' manuals. I. Title.

TH8531.F37 2008
698--dc22   2007024075

President/CEO: Ken Fund
Vice President for Sales & Marketing: Kevin Hamric

Home Improvement Group

Publisher: Bryan Trandem
Managing Editor: Tracy Stanley
Senior Editor: Mark Johanson
Editor: Jennifer Gehlhar

Creative Director: Michele Lanci-Altomare
Senior Design Manager: Brad Springer
Design Managers: Jon Simpson, Mary Rohl

Director of Photography: Tim Himsel
Lead Photographer: Steve Galvin
Photo Coordinator: Joanne Wawra
Shop Manager: Bryan McLain

Production Managers: Linda Halls, Laura Hokkanen

Author: Jerri Farris
Page Layout Artist: Danielle Smith
Photographers: Andrea Rugg, Joel Schnell
Shop Help: Dan Anderson, Tami Helmer, John Webb

The Complete Guide to Decorating with Ceramic Tile
Created by: The Editors of Creative Publishing international, Inc., in cooperation with Black & Decker.
Black & Decker® is a trademark of The Black & Decker Corporation and is used under license.

NOTICE TO READERS

For safety, use caution, care, and good judgment when following the procedures described in this book. The Publisher and Black & Decker cannot assume responsibility for any damage to property or injury to persons as a result of misuse of the information provided.

The techniques shown in this book are general techniques for various applications. In some instances, additional techniques not shown in this book may be required. Always follow manufacturers' instructions included with products, since deviating from the directions may void warranties. The projects in this book vary widely as to skill levels required: some may not be appropriate for all do-it-yourselfers, and some may require professional help.

Consult your local Building Department for information on building permits, codes, and other laws as they apply to your project.

Contents

The Complete Guide to
Decorating with Ceramic Tile

Introduction

Tile is a natural, logical choice if you're looking for a floorcovering that's beautiful, durable, affordable, and easy to install yourself. Whether it's ceramic, porcelain, natural stone, glass, or metal, virtually all tile begins with materials mined from the earth.

Before we get into the many reasons for tile's popularity, let's take a look at its history. The first tile made of fired-clay was produced before recorded history. That's right—before recorded history. Someone must have noticed that wet clay hardened when it dried. And someone else must have figured out that clay hardened even more when it was heated. It wasn't much of a leap from there to realize that higher temperatures produced harder tile.

Estimates vary regarding the first use of tile, but archaeologists have discovered a kiln near Sienna, Italy, believed to date from the 3rd century B.C. Some scientists believe that Egyptians used colored glazes on fired clay more than 6,000 years ago. Tile has been found in the pyramids and in the ruins of Babylon and of ancient Greek cities. Intact tile has even been found in the excavation of Pompeii. Pretty remarkable considering that it was buried in ash for 2,000 years.

Alternating taupe and white squares form an attractive border around this rustic sitting room.

Although it's impossible to trace the very first use of tile, there's no doubt that by the Middle Ages, handmade tile graced the walls and floors of hundreds—if not thousands—of important public buildings across the known world. By the 17th century, the production of tile was so important to its economy that England developed strict manufacturing standards and set stiff penalties for violating them. By the 1800s, newer, more efficient manufacturing processes brought down prices and tile began to be used in homes as well as less extravagant religious and public buildings.

Today, tile is installed in homes and commercial buildings on every continent, probably because it makes sense in so many settings. What other material is so versatile? Tile can be smooth or rough, intricate or simple, colorful or muted. It provides excellent insulation, doesn't give off toxic fumes in a fire, resists fading, and repels moisture. In fact, tile rated as impervious is so easy to clean that it's often used on walls and floors in commercial food preparation areas and operating rooms.

Small squares set on the diagonal become diamonds to accent the corners of large square tiles.

Within a mosaic border, rectangles in alternating colors are set to form an unusual but surprisingly uncomplicated pattern.

Designers say the single best thing about tile is its versatility: It can make rooms seem larger or more intimate, brighter or cozier, grandly formal or uniquely artistic. The key to producing these illusions is creating a design and a layout that emphasizes certain elements of a room and minimizes others. For example, putting a broad border of light tile at the top of a wall can make a ceiling seem higher, just as putting dark tile around the perimeter of a large room can make it appear to be more cozy. Changing the size or pattern of the tile in an area, such as a shower or a kitchen backsplash, marks that area as special or important.

This kitchen and eating area showcases a spectacular floor produced from black and cream squares and rectangles highlighted by golden squares set on the diagonal. An elaborate design like this requires very careful planning, but it's set using the same simple principles as any other floor.

Another great benefit of tile is the ease with which it can be sued for decorative projects. From kitchen countertops to picture frames and coffee tabletops, tile offers unlimited design options and ample opportunities to showcase your creativity.

Once you understand the basics, you can lay tile almost anywhere—the process remains very much the same no matter what the project may be. The fun—and more challenging part—of a tile project is creating the design and layout, and that's what we're going to emphasize throughout this book. First, we'll give you plenty of information on tile of every variety and then we'll talk about the design process itself. A review of layout procedures completes that section.

Broken tile and decorative bits form a colorful mosaic behind this display of glassware. Dark grout emphasizes the shapes and movement of the mosaic.

The natural color variations and diagonal set of these stone tiles provide a nice counterpoint to the simple color palette and straight lines of this dining room.

Next, we'll present a range of projects, each with plenty of clear photographs and thorough step-by-step instructions that can be adapted to your specific projects. At the beginning of each project chapter you'll find several pages of photos that should inspire you and maybe even provide direction for your own dreams and schemes.

Finally, you'll find the background information necessary for success. This section starts with the removal of current floor and wall coverings and moves through the planning process and into the nitty gritty of setting tile. You'll find information on the tools and materials you'll need, too. Read this information before purchasing materials or selecting tile. It should help cut down on aggravation and extra trips to the store.

Ready? Let's get started.

Small mosaic tile in two colors provides a dramatic backdrop for a contemporary entryway.

With a view like this, the best design is one that gets out of its own way. This blue mosaic tile echoes the color of the mountains without competing for attention.

Selecting Tile

Like any other building materials, not all tile is created equal. Some types that work beautifully on a wall wouldn't withstand daily foot traffic; some glossy, glazed styles would be treacherous on a floor, especially a floor in a wet area. The only answer to this puzzle is to learn all you can about the various materials and styles of tile as you begin planning a project.

This chapter describes and illustrates the differences between floor and wall tile, as well as tile made from materials such as ceramic, porcelain, glass, metal, and natural stone, among others. You'll find dozens of examples of tile installed in kitchens, bathrooms, entries, and living areas as well as a glossary of basic tile facts.

Take time to read this chapter and evaluate the varieties of tile that may (or may not) be appropriate for the projects you've got under consideration. Armed with this information, you'll be better prepared to select tile that will serve you well for many years to come.

In This Chapter:

- Floors
- Walls
- Kitchens
- Bathrooms
- Entries
- Living Areas
- Tile Facts

Floors

Floor tile needs to be more than just attractive—it needs to be strong and durable as well. After all, floors bear the weight of furniture and foot traffic, not to mention the sudden impact of every one and every thing that falls on them. Floor tile is engineered to tolerate these stresses. Most floor tile is also suitable for countertops. And although it's generally thicker and heavier than wall tile, many styles of floor tile can be used on walls. The trim pieces necessary for counters and walls aren't always available, though, which may limit your options.

When shopping for tile, look for ratings by the American National Standards Institute or the Porcelain Enamel Institute (see page 13). If ratings aren't available, check with your dealer to make sure the tile you're considering is suitable for your project.

Before you start shopping, consider where the tile will be used and what you want it to accomplish. Will it be exposed to moisture? Should it be a focal point or a subtle background? Do you want it to establish the room's color scheme or blend into it? The range of options is truly mind-boggling. Establishing some guidelines before you go shopping will simplify the selection process enormously.

Muted colors and a subtle design provide an attractive background for the interesting architectural features and accessories of this entry.

These large, plain square tiles complement the shape of the windows, vent hood, and hanging rack. Repeating a motif from the room is always a successful strategy.

Floor Tile Ratings ▸

Floor tile often comes labeled with water absorption and PEI (Porcelain Enamel Institute) ratings. Absorption is a concern because tile that soaks up water is susceptible to mildew and mold and can be difficult to clean. Ratings indicate how a tile can be used and whether or not it needs to be sealed against moisture. Tile is rated non-vitreous, semi-vitreous, vitreous, or impervious, in increasing order of water resistance. Non-vitreous tile is quite porous; semi-vitreous is used in dry-to-occasionally-wet locations; vitreous tile can be used without regard to its exposure to moisture. Impervious tile generally is reserved for restaurants, hospitals, and commercial applications where sanitation is a special concern.

The PEI number is a wear rating that indicates how the tile should be used. Ratings of 1 and 2 indicate tile is suitable for walls only; tile rated 3 and 4 is suitable for all residential applications—walls, counters, and floors. Most tile carries absorption and PEI ratings, but some—especially imported and art tiles—may not. Ask the retailer if you're not sure.

Depending on the retailer, tile may also have other ratings. Some tile is graded 1 to 3 for the quality of manufacturing. Grade 1 indicates standard grade; 2 indicates minor glaze and size flaws; 3 indicates major flaws; use for decoration only. Tile suitable for outdoor use is sometimes rated with regard to its resistance to frost. Finally, coefficient of friction numbers may be included with some tile. The higher the coefficient, the more slip resistant the tile. A dry coefficient of .6 is the minimum standard for the Americans with Disabilities Act.

Walls

Wall tile, unlike floor tile, doesn't have the burden of bearing weight or withstanding heavy traffic, so it can be thinner, have finer finishes, and, in some cases, be less expensive. Wall tile layouts tend to have more exposed edges, so manufacturers often offer matching trim and border pieces with finished edges. Wall tile is generally self spacing—individual tiles have small flanges on each edge to help keep the spacing even. You can use floor tile on walls, but since it is heavier, it tends to slide down during installation. Using battens while installing can help solve this problem. Fewer styles of matching trim tile are available for floor tile, which may make it difficult to conceal unfinished edges.

Wall tile should not be used on floors or countertops, however, because it will not stand up to much weight or sharp impacts. If you have concerns about a tile's suitability, ask your retailer or look for ratings by the American National Standards Institute or the Porcelain Enamel Institute. Wall tile can be a fairly inconspicuous wall covering or, if used in an elaborate design, it can become the focal point of a room. As with floor tiles, there are styles for every effect from subtle to bold, so envision the effect you want before you head to the tile store or home improvement center.

Even plain wall tile in solid colors makes a bold statement when combined with accessories in similar or complementary colors.

Borders liven up walls and break up otherwise boring expanses of solid color.

Wall Tile Ratings ▶

Most tile intended for walls comes labeled with a water absorption rating. As with floor tile, absorbent wall tile will be susceptible to mildew and mold and be difficult to clean. Tiles are rated non-vitreous, semi-vitreous, vitreous, and impervious, in increasing order of water resistance. Practically speaking, these ratings tell you whether your tile may require sealant or if it can be left as is. Non-vitreous and semi-vitreous do absorb noticeable amounts of water and may need to be sealed in damp rooms like bathrooms. Sealant can alter a tile's appearance, so test before you buy.

There are a few other ratings to consider when purchasing wall tile. Depending on where you buy tile, it may be graded from 1 to 3 for the quality of manufacturing. Grade 1 indicates standard grade, suitable for all installations. Second grade indicates minor glaze and size flaws, but the tile is structurally standard. Grade 3 tiles may be slightly irregular in shape and are decorative, suitable only for walls. Tiles with manufacturing irregularities may be more difficult to lay out and install precisely. If you live in a freeze zone and are looking for tile for outdoor walls, you'll also want tile rated resistant to frost. If the frost-resistance rating is not on the package, the retailer should be able to tell you. Some colored tile may come with a graphic to indicate the degree of color variation from tile to tile—and in most cases it does vary somewhat.

Kitchens

Impervious to moisture and stains and very close to maintenance free, tile is an excellent choice for nearly every surface in a kitchen—from the floors to the walls to the countertops. Almost anything goes. Choose glass, natural stone, metal, porcelain—any tile that suits your taste and the style of your home can be put to work in the kitchen.

This stone floor mingles with stone countertops and stainless steel appliances in a kitchen fit for a true chef.

Spills happen, especially in kitchens. Polished stone makes an impressive kitchen floor, but only if the stone isn't slippery when wet. Porcelain with an impressed texture and nonslip glaze may be a better choice—it can provide the look without the hazard.

Variations in the setting pattern and a mosaic border around the center island provide touches of texture and color.

Tumbled stone blends this backsplash into the background, allowing the rich wood tones of the cabinets to shine. Choose stone that has been finished or apply sealer to repel stains and water. If no trim tile is available for the stone tile you've chosen, polish the cut edges to create your own.

Mosaic tile—small, colorful tiles made of ceramic, porcelain, terra-cotta or cement—can be installed on walls and floors to form patterns and pictures or just to add a splash of color. Mosaic tile can be expensive, but covering the few square feet of a backsplash, such as this one, creates exciting decoration at a reasonable price.

Glass tile is available in a variety of colors and degrees of translucency, as well as shapes and sizes. Two different sizes and a variety of colors grace the walls of this kitchen. All glass tile is translucent to some degree, so it's important to use a white tile adhesive that won't affect the appearance of the finished installation. Glass tile can be scratched and cracked, so avoid using it on walls in areas that will be subjected to constant bumps and scrapes, such as behind doors.

Art tile ranges from original, hand-painted mosaics to tiles that are individually shaped and formed by hand. They make wonderful accents because just a few eye-catching tiles will give a wall a distinctive look. Because these tiles are generally hand crafted, they can be less durable and resistant to scratches and moisture than other tile. They should be used only in areas where they will not be subject to excessive wear and tear or moisture.

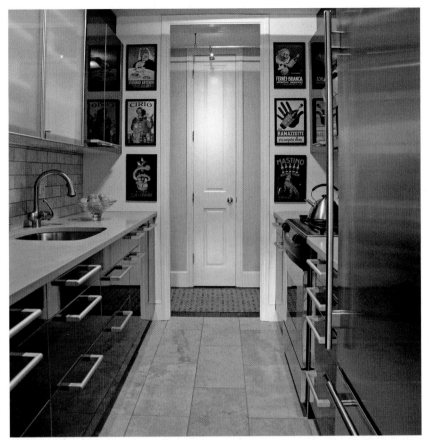

The stone subway tile on the backsplash and large rectangular floor tile draw the eye through this galley kitchen.

Glazed tile adds color and protects the walls between this cooktop and vent hood. In areas that will be exposed to cooking grease and moisture, such as a backsplash behind a cooktop or grilling area, glazed tile is highly appropriate because it's so easy to clean.

Bathrooms

Bathrooms and tile are made for each other. The natural elements of bathing—water, steam, and heat—can destroy many materials over time, but not tile. Well-maintained tile will stand up to it all for decades.

Textured, slip-resistant tile reduces the danger of falling on wet floors. Some types of tile, such as tumbled stone, have natural texture; other types have textures molded into or added to the surface. Whatever tile you choose for bathroom floors, be sure it is both water- and slip-resistant.

Almost anything goes when it comes to wall tile in bathrooms. As long as they're water- and stain-resistant or can be treated to be so, you can choose any style your heart desires.

This combination of translucent glass and white ceramic tile creates a clean, contemporary background for this sleek bathroom.

Bands of color transform this bathroom into a cheerful oasis. The magenta bands on the partition wall are aligned with the bands of the background wall. Such strategic placement is crucial when combining a variety of colors and shapes.

This bathroom incorporates several colors and styles of ceramic tile. The floor has large tiles while the walls feature metallic tiles in various sizes. The back wall tiles are laid out in a staggered running-bond pattern. The front wall features accent tiles that have decorative imprints. The varied patterns work because the colors are similar and muted.

Metallic glazes create slightly reflective surfaces that are particularly suited to contemporary rooms.

Decorative tiles can be mixed with plain to produce stunning designs like this one. Many manufacturers will customize tile with photographs that you choose or provide. Craft stores also offer kits that allow you to add your own photographs to tile.

Natural stone can be custom cut to fit a tub surround such as this one. Because stone is a natural material, you need to expect variations in color, texture, and markings—they're part of the charm. You also need to understand that (with the exception of granite), stone tends to be quite porous and requires periodic sealing to prevent stains. Not all types of stone are scratch resistant, either, so it's important to understand the qualities of the stone you're considering for a bathroom.

Subway tile, simple rectangular tile, blends the shower into its surroundings. The room is brightened considerably by a backsplash of colorful mosaic tile. A niche, cleverly sized and placed, creates the appearance that the backsplash continues behind the shower, and mosaic floor provides a visual anchor.

Stones cut to resemble river rocks make an unusual bathroom floor. The stones, which are attached to a mesh backing, are remarkably easy to install. Coordinating grout blends the tiles; contrasting grout would emphasize the individual stones.

Border tiles, set in a rather random fashion, create a focal point behind the counter and sinks in this colorful bathroom. Don't limit your use of decorative tiles like these to conventional methods. Let your imagination run free—you may come up with your own unique take on their possibilities.

Entries

Entries are hardworking spaces, often exposed to more dirt and moisture than the rest of the house. When selecting tile for entry floors, make sure it's slip resistant (even when wet) and scratch resistant as well as attractive and easy to clean.

Mosaic tile, with its multitude of grout lines, is highly slip-resistant. A border defines the edges of this hallway and leads the eye toward the next room.

Mosaic designs lend themselves to replicating area rugs, such as the design shown here. When placing such a design in an entry, placement is crucial. The tile should be installed exactly as a rug would be placed, centered within the open area. Designs like this one are a combination of field tile and border tile, each attached to mesh backing for easy installation. It's easiest to install the tile if the design requires an even number of field tile. If tile must be trimmed, be sure to trim both sides equally so the design remains centered and even.

Large tile produces fewer grout joints, which tends to visually expand a small or narrow space, such as this entry. This tiled wall niche, built to showcase collections, adds interest to the otherwise plain entry.

Living Areas

In living areas, tile generally acts as a backdrop more than the focus of the room. Still, borders, mosaics, and decorative pieces add style and interest to a room.

Floor warming systems are especially welcome in these rooms, keeping the floor toasty during even the coldest weather.

The tiled wall provides an artful focal point for this ultra-sleek seating area.

Contrasting grout emphasizes the unusual setting pattern in this dining room floor.

The green glass tile of this fireplace surround complements the treasured collection displayed on the mantle.

Tile Facts

Not all tiles are right for all installations. The discussions here are designed to help you select the most appropriate tile for your projects.

Porcelain tile is produced by pressing refined clay into shape and then firing it in a kiln at very high temperatures. The resulting tile is extremely hard, absorbs very little or no water, and doesn't stain or mildew. Porcelain tile is manufactured in all shapes and sizes, and, because its white base color accepts dye beautifully, a virtually unlimited range of colors and finishes are available. Tile makers can also imprint textures when the tile is pressed, giving them slip-resistant surfaces well suited for floors in wet locations. Porcelain tile is colored by mixing dye into the clay rather than applying it in a glaze, which means the color extends through the full thickness of the tile. This process also means that tile makers can press finer, more intricate textures and patterns into the tile. Porcelain tile can even be pressed so that it's nearly indistinguishable from cut stone, which tends to be more expensive but less durable. For ease of care, porcelain is hard to beat. Its smooth finish and imperviousness to moisture keep soil and stains from setting in, making it easy to maintain. *Note: grout can stain porous material, so take great care in grouting and be sure to follow manufacturer instructions.*

Glazed ceramic tile is made from clay pressed into a shape by a machine, glazed, and then fired in a kiln. The glaze, made up of a number of glass and metal elements, provides color and creates a hard, shiny surface. To make floor tile slip-resistant, the surface is textured or given a slightly raised design; on others the glaze itself includes materials added to create a non-skid surface. Glazed tile generally absorbs very little or no water, making it both easy to maintain and mildew resistant. If the glaze is hard and scratch-resistant and the tile is properly installed and maintained, glazed ceramic tile can last for decades.

Glass tile is an especially interesting option for walls, although in some applications in can be used on floors as well. It is available in a variety of colors and degrees of translucency, as well as shapes and sizes. Because most glass tile is translucent to some degree, it's important to use a white tile adhesive that won't affect the appearance of the tiles once they are installed. Glass is impervious to moisture, but it can be scratched and cracked, so it shouldn't be installed where it will get hit by swinging doors or scratched by general traffic.

Metal tiles are quite expensive per square foot, but adding just a few to an installation of glazed or porcelain tiles can have a big impact. Metal tiles are installed just like standard tiles, and they are available in shapes and thicknesses to work in most layouts. They are available with smooth finishes, polished or unpolished, and with embossed designs. Some metals may weather and discolor with time and exposure to moisture.

Natural stone tile includes marble, granite, slate, and other more exotic stones cut very precisely into tiles of various sizes that can be installed just like manufactured tile. Because stone is a natural material, variations in color, texture, and markings must be expected. Manufacturers do offer stone tiles with some added finish, though. In addition to polished, suppliers offer a variety of distressed and textured finishes that can be very attractive as well as slip-resistant. With the exception of granite, natural stone tends to be quite porous and requires periodic sealing to prevent staining. Also, not all types are uniformly abrasion-resistant, so check before making a purchase. Some stone is so soft that it can be very easily scratched by normal use. Refer to note at end of porcelain tile entry (page 32).

Terra-cotta tile evokes images of rustic patios in Mexico or perhaps sunny piazzas on the Mediterranean. These images are quite appropriate because terra-cotta tile originated in these regions. The tile is traditionally made by pressing unrefined clay into molds of various shapes and firing it (terra-cotta literally means "baked earth"). The color of the tile, from brown to red to yellow, is largely a result of the minerals unique to the local soil. Machine-made terra-cotta tile is regular in shape and can be laid like standard tile, but traditional terra-cotta, especially handmade Mexican saltillo tile, has irregularities and uneven shapes and thus requires more care during installation. The variability and rustic character of the tile make up much of its appeal—and they make terra-cotta quite slip-resistant. Unglazed terra-cotta, which is porous and absorbent, should be treated with sealant before being used in wet locations.

Modern quarry tile is made from red clay extruded through a dye that makes it resemble cut stone. The dye also creates a ribbed back on the tile to improve mortar adhesion. The rough-hewn aspect of quarry tile makes it visually appealing and slip-resistant, but the open texture increases maintenance requirements. Quarry tile is often much more absorbent than glazed or porcelain tile, making it more prone to stains and mildew (see note at end of porcelain tile entry on page 32). Sealants must be added to increase this tile's durability and serviceability.

Mosaic tiles are ceramic, porcelain, terra-cotta, stone, or other tile cut into small pieces. Individual small tiles are often mounted on a mesh backing so that large squares of many tiles can be installed at once. These squares may be a solid color or contain a pattern or image. Individual mosaic tiles are also available for making custom accents and mosaics. Mosaic tile can be very low maintenance or it can require periodic application of sealant, depending on the materials. Mosaic tile is generally quite slip-resistant because of the large number of grout lines in an installation.

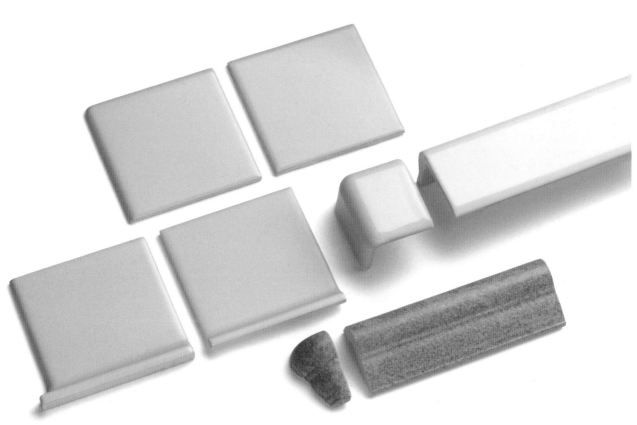

Cement body tiles are actually shaped pieces of concrete. They can be made in nearly endless colors and textures because cement can be dyed, coated, and molded quite easily. It can even be finished to take on the appearance of marble or other stone. Cement tile can also be pressed with pronounced raised or relief designs. Cement tile is an economical choice both for its low cost and great durability, but there are several factors to keep in mind. Unfinished cement tile is highly porous and stains very easily. This also means that some cement tile is unsuitable for outdoor installations, as it may crack if it freezes. Cement tile should be treated periodically with a sealant to preserve its appearance and prevent mildew.

Accent tiles add visual interest in the form of borders and outlines. Many, many varieties are available as wall tile, which typically include painted or molded patterns and often are slightly thicker than field tile.

Trim tiles are designed to conceal exposed edges of field tile, especially on wall and counter installations. Bull nose tile is used to finish the edges of partial walls; cove and corner tile shields curves and corners; chair rail tile accents a wall of field tile or functions as an accent around edges. When planning a wall project, investigate available trim as part of the planning process.

Design & Layout for Tile Projects

The process of actually setting tile is a simple one. The real challenge—and much of the fun—comes in designing a project. This is the heart of the matter, the element that elevates a project from acceptable to professional quality.

As you plan a project, allow plenty of time for this design stage. It is a very creative process; an opportunity to consider colors, textures, layouts, and finishing methods. If trim tiles are necessary, calculate how many and what styles you'll need and evaluate how and where they'll be used.

This chapter guides you through experimenting with ideas, measuring accurately, and testing layouts for floor and wall projects. You'll find information to help you center the layout within the room and minimize the number of tiles that have to be cut. You'll also find information on how best to handle corners, borders, and trim pieces.

In these pages we'll show you how to establish reference lines for floor and wall projects, how to negotiate around obstacles, and how to deal with rooms that aren't square or walls that aren't plumb.

In This Chapter:

- Laying Out Floor Designs
- Laying Out Wall Designs

Laying Out Floor Designs

Once you have a stable, firm, smooth substrate in place (see pages 218 to 225), the next step is laying out the project. While it might be tempting to go directly to laying the tile, resist the temptation. Planning is a very important step in the process and one that pays off in the long run. There are few things more frustrating than running into issues that could have been avoided through a little more attention to detail on the front end.

A tile floor essentially is a giant grid, and imperfections can be quite obvious, especially if the grout contrasts sharply with the tile.

Good layouts start with accurate measurements and detailed scale drawings. Use these drawings to experiment with potential layouts until you're satisfied. Try to:

- Center the tile within the room and keep the final tiles at opposite sides equal in size.
- Minimize the number of cuts required.
- Disguise disparities in rooms that are not square.

Laying out borders, diagonal sets, or running bonds involves a few special considerations that are also discussed in the following pages.

Drawing Layouts for Floor Designs

It's not necessary to draw layouts for projects in small, square rooms with no tricky issues. On the other hand, drawings are helpful for projects in rooms that have more than four corners or are more than an inch out of square, and for projects that involve several adjacent rooms.

To start, measure the room. Figure out a scale that's easy to use—one square per tile for larger-scale graph paper or four squares per tile on smaller-scale graph paper—and draw the room. Make several copies of the drawing so you can experiment with layouts without redoing it.

Next, lay out at least 10 tiles with spacers and measure them. Add the thickness of one grout line and divide the total by 10 to calculate the exact size of one tile with grout. Using this calculation and the same

scale as you used for the room diagram, draw layouts until you find one that works. Sometimes there's no way to avoid narrow tiles at the edges. In that case, plan to put them along the least visible wall in the room or in areas that will be covered with furniture or fixtures.

Confirm your calculations by testing the layout. No matter how careful you are, it's possible to make mistakes when you're working with drawings and measurements. It's much better to discover any miscalculations before setting any tile or spreading any mortar. Lay out one complete row of full-sized tile in at least two directions. Adjust the layout as necessary.

If the layout is complicated or involves lots of cuts, it's worth the time to dry-fit the entire floor.

How to Test Corners for Square

To get accurate room measurements, start in a corner of the room and measure along the wall to the opposite corner. Do this for each wall, writing down the measurements as you go. When measuring to locate permanent obstacles or fixtures, pick a point and take all measurements from it. That way you'll have a constant reference point when you diagram the room.

Check for square by measuring a corner. On one wall, mark a spot 3 feet from the corner; on the other wall, mark a spot 4 feet from the corner. Measure between the marks. If the distance between the marks is exactly 5 feet, the room is square. For greater accuracy in larger rooms, use multiples of 3, 4, and 5 such as 6, 8, and 10, or 9, 12, and 15.

How to Lay Out Floor Designs

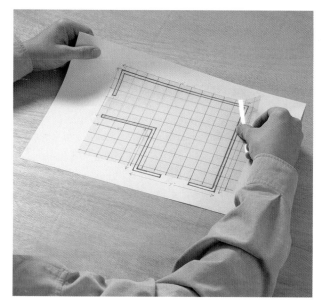

Diagram the entire room, drawing it to scale including any permanent fixtures such as cabinets and stairways. Draw possible tile layouts, at the same scale as your room drawing, on transparency paper and place them over the room diagram. Experiment with layouts until you find a successful arrangement.

Make a story stick to help you estimate how many tiles will fit in a given area. Lay out a row of tile, with spacers, and set an 8-ft.-long 1 × 2 next to it. (Position the end of the 1 × 2 in the center of a grout line.) Holding the board in place, mark the edges of each grout line.

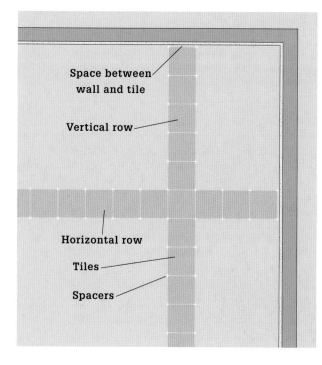

Space between
wall and tile

Vertical row

Horizontal row

Tiles

Spacers

Test the layout by setting out one vertical and one horizontal row of tile, all the way to the walls in both directions.

Dry-lay the tile if you're working with a complex layout, tiling around a series of obstacles, or setting tiles on the diagonal. You may find that you need to shift the layout slightly to keep from cutting very small tile for edges or corners.

Establishing Reference Lines for Floor Designs

Reference lines are used as guides for the first tiles laid. Before you snap these lines, think about where to start tiling. The goal is to work it out so that you don't need to step on recently laid tile in order to continue working. It often makes sense to start in the middle of a room, but not always—sometimes it's better to start a few feet from a wall and work your way across the room. If a room has only one door, start at the far end and move toward the door. Give some thought to the issue and make sure you don't tile yourself into a corner!

Another way to help keep the tile straight is by using a batten, which is nothing more than a long, straight board used as a guide. A piece of plywood works well if you maintain the factory edge. Just position the board and tack it in place, using several screws. Butt the first row of tile up to it and leave it in place until the mortar starts to dry. Remove the batten and continue setting tile. Maintaining even spacing will maintain the straight lines.

How to Mark Reference Lines for Straight Sets

Position a reference line (X) by measuring between opposite sides of the room and marking the center of each side. Snap a chalk line between these marks.

Measure and mark the centerpoint of the chalk line. From this point, use a framing square to establish a second line perpendicular to the first. Snap a second reference line (Y) across the room.

How to Mark Reference Lines for Diagonal Sets

Snap reference lines that meet in the exact center of the room. Make sure the lines are perpendicular, then mark a point on each line precisely the same distance from the center.

Snap lines to connect the marked points. The sides of the resulting square will be tilted at a 45° angle to the room. Use the square to create working lines for laying out the room.

How to Mark Reference Lines for Running Bond Sets

Snap perpendicular reference lines as described on page 41. Dry-fit a few tiles side by side, using spacers. Offset the rows by a measurement that's equal to one-half the length of the tile and one-half the width of the grout line. Measure the total width of the dry-fitted section.

Use this measurement to snap a series of equally spaced parallel lines to help keep your tiles straight during installation. (Running-bond layouts are most effective with rectangular tiles.)

Planning Borders & Design Areas

A border can divide a floor into sections or it can define a design area such as the one shown at right. You can create a design inside the border by merely turning the tiles at a 45° angle, by installing decorative tiles, or by creating a mosaic such as the one shown on pages 74 to 78. Such designs should cover between 25 and 50 percent of the floor. If the design is too small, it'll get lost in the floor. If it's too big, it'll be distracting.

Determine the size and location of the border on graph paper, then transfer those measurements onto the floor. A dry run with the border and field tile is essential.

The tile is installed in three stages. The border is placed first, followed by outside field tile, then the tile within the border.

How to Lay Out a Border

Measure the length and width of the room in which you'll be installing the border.

Transfer the measurements onto paper by making a scale drawing of the room. Include the locations of cabinets, doors, permanent fixtures, and furniture.

(continued)

3

Determine the size of the border you want. Bordered designs should be between ¼ and ½ the area of the room. Draw the border on transparency paper, using the same scale as the room drawing.

4

Place the transparency of the border over the room drawing. Move it around to find the best layout. Tape the border transparency in place over the room drawing. Draw perpendicular lines through the center of the border and calculate the distance from the center lines to the border.

5

Transfer the measurements from the border transparency onto your floor, starting with your center lines. Snap chalk lines to establish your layout for the border.

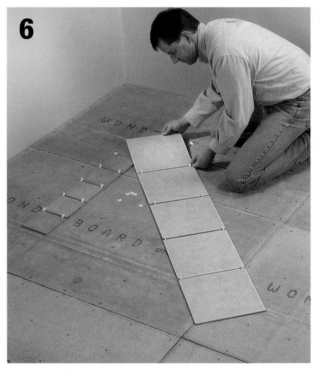

6

Lay out the border along the reference lines in a dry run. Do a dry run of the field tiles inside and outside of the border along the center lines. Make any adjustments, if necessary.

Laying Out Wall Designs

Wall projects can be challenging because walls are so rarely plumb and true. In some cases, that means the walls themselves need to be adjusted before the tile portion of the project begins. Most of the time, though, it simply means being aware of the issues and working around them as discussed in the following pages. (If your walls need work before you begin tiling them, consult pages 240 to 249 for ideas and information.)

Layout is critical to successful wall projects. Start with accurate measurements and draw the room to scale.

Use the drawing to experiment with potential arrangements. The goal is to arrive at a layout that gives the walls a balanced, symmetrical look.

- Center the tile within the room and keep the final tiles at opposite sides equal in size.
- Minimize the number of cuts required and avoid cutting very narrow pieces of tile.
- Disguise disparities on walls that are not square.
- Plan effective placement of borders, liners, and trim.

Drawing Layouts for Wall Designs

It may not be necessary to draw layouts for small, simple projects, but it's a good idea if you're tiling more than one wall, creating designs or borders, or working with walls that aren't plumb or a room that's out of square by more than an inch. Start by checking to see whether the walls are plumb. Place a carpenter's level along the edge of a straight board, then place the board against the walls and on the floor at the bottom of the walls. If a wall is out of square by more than ¼" per 8 feet, you'll need to add moldings, build up the wall with joint compound, or trim the tiles in a way that makes the imperfection less obvious. (See pages 240 to 243 for details.) Check outside corners for plumb and make careful note of any problems.

Now, measure and draw the walls on graph paper, including windows, doors, and permanent fixtures such as bathtubs. (Figure out a scale that's easy to use—one square per tile for larger-scale graph paper or four squares per tile on smaller-scale graph paper.) Make several copies of the drawing so you can experiment with layouts without redrawing it.

Double check the size of your tile, including borders or accent tiles, and begin evaluating layouts. The goal is to make the room look balanced and to place cut tile in the least visible positions. For example, if the height of a wall above a sink or bathtub can't be covered in full tile, it's best to put cut tile on the bottom row so that the top row (which is more visible) is composed of full tile. If you're adding accents, position them so that the repeating pattern is even or at least balanced across the wall.

How to Draw a Tile Layout for Wall Designs

1

Check the walls and corners to see if they're plumb. Make any adjustments necessary before beginning your tile project.

2

Measure the walls, paying particular attention to the placement of windows, doors, and permanent fixtures. Use these measurements to create a scale drawing of each wall to be tiled.

Lay out your tiles, accents, and trim. Take measurements of the tile layout.

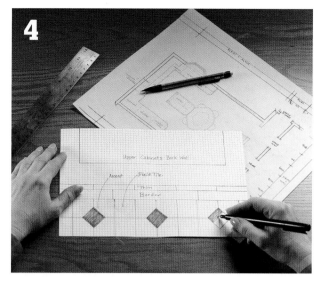

Draw your tile layout to scale on the wall drawing to establish your reference lines.

Testing Wall Layouts

Establishing perpendicular reference lines is a critical part of every tile project, including wall projects. To create these lines, measure and mark the midpoint at the top and bottom of the wall, and then again along each side. Snap chalk lines between opposite marks to create your vertical and horizontal centerlines. Use the 3-4-5 triangle method to make sure the lines are drawn correctly (see page 39). Adjust the lines until they are exactly perpendicular.

Next, do a dry run of your proposed layout, starting at the center of the wall and working toward an adjoining wall. If the gap between the last full tile and the wall is too narrow, adjust your starting point. Continue to dry-fit tile along the walls, paying special attention to any windows, doors, or permanent fixtures in the wall. If you end up with very narrow tiles anywhere, adjust the reference lines (and your layout) to avoid them. It's best not to cut tiles by more than half.

If your wall has an outside corner, start your dry run there. Place bullnose tiles over the edges of the adjoining field tiles. If this results in a narrow gap at the opposite wall, install trimmed tile next to the bullnose edge to even out or avoid the gap.

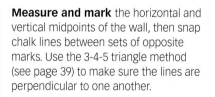

Measure and mark the horizontal and vertical midpoints of the wall, then snap chalk lines between sets of opposite marks. Use the 3-4-5 triangle method (see page 39) to make sure the lines are perpendicular to one another.

How to Test a Wall Layout

Attach a batten to the wall along your horizontal reference line, using screws. Dry-fit tiles on the batten, aligning the middle tile with the vertical centerline.

If you end up with too narrow a gap along the wall in step 1, move over half the width of a tile by centering the middle tile over the vertical centerline.

Use a story stick (see page 40) to determine whether your planned layout works vertically. If necessary, adjust the size of the first row of tile.

Dry-fit the first row of tile, then hold a story stick along the horizontal guideline with one grout line matched to the vertical reference line. Mark the grout lines, which will correspond with the grout lines of the first row and can be used as reference points.

How to Work Around Outside Corners

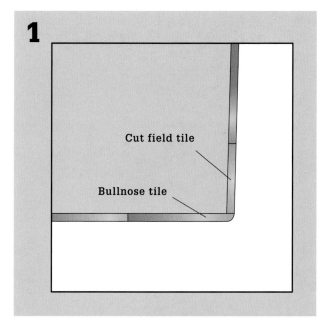

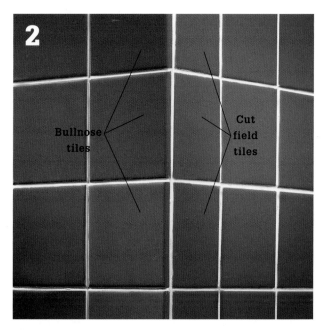

Overlap field tiles with bullnose tiles on outside corners. Try to use whole tiles on the corner, but if that's not possible, plan to trim the field tiles. If the wall is slightly out of plumb and not very wide, line up the bullnose tiles so they overlap the field tiles evenly.

Disguise walls that are badly out of plumb by installing the field tile on that side, trimming them as necessary. Overlap the cut edges with bullnose tiles. Install tiles on both walls at the same time, making sure the bullnose pieces cover the cut edges.

How to Work Around Windows

Use a story stick to evaluate the layout around obstacles, such as windows. Adjust reference lines as necessary to avoid cutting tiles by more than half, either vertically or horizontally.

Remove aprons (on windows that have them) and tile up to the window, then replace the trim. Aprons are the only window trim that can be removed and replaced in this manner.

Floor Projects

We start the project portion of the book with a basic floor project, which is probably the most common tile project undertaken by homeowners. This chapter walks you through a basic installation, and then branches out to illustrate how to set a running bond tile pattern, a diagonal pattern within a border, and how to set hexagonal tile.

With these basic tile-setting techniques in hand, you'll be ready to set mosaic floor tile and even to create an original mosaic design. Finally, we present the installation of a custom-tiled shower base, an advanced but completely realistic project for a do-it-yourselfer.

A floor typically is the largest single surface in a room and so plays a major role in establishing the style of the total room. Neutral or dramatic, plain or elaborate, these projects present the techniques necessary for just about any design you can find or dream up.

In This Chapter:

- Installing a Tile Floor
- Installing a Stone & Mosaic Tile Floor
- Installing a Glass Mosaic Floor
- Installing an Original Mosaic Design
- Building a Tiled Shower Base

Natural stone tile floors range from extremely formal and elegant to casual. Set in combination with decorative tile, this natural stone tile floor presents a rustic atmosphere in a western-style home.

Informal and earthy, terra-cotta can be recognized by its characteristic color and texture. Machine-made tile is consistent in size and shape, but handmade tile includes a wide range of shapes and textures.

Durable and practical, cement body tile is also economical and attractive. It should be periodically sealed to maintain its appearance.

Combining mosaic tile in a variety of colors and sizes produces elegant designs. Elaborate patterns can be deceptively easy to create with tile mounted to mesh backings. Even pre-arranged borders are widely available. Mosaic tile of any material is generally quite slip-resistant because of the many grout lines.

Terra-cotta ("baked earth") tile is made by pressing unrefined clay into molds and baking it. Its color is a result of the minerals unique to the soil from which it is made. Machine-made terra-cotta tile can be laid like standard tile, but traditional terra-cotta, with its irregularities and uneven shapes, requires more care during installation. Unglazed terra-cotta, which is porous and absorbent, should be treated with sealant before being installed in potentially wet locations, such as entries.

Tile walls flow into tile floors when connected by borders, liners, and baseboard tile. When shopping for tile for an installation like this one, investigate the available trim tile and make a detailed plan for the installation.

The tile floor and walls work with the furnishings to provide the illusion of a European villa in this suburban foyer.

In a large room, tile can be used to define functional spaces. In this contemporary living room, a conversation area is set apart by a border and change of setting pattern.

The multitude of grout lines makes mosaic tile naturally slip-resistant, a wonderful quality for bathroom floors. The light, slightly uneven tones in this mosaic floor make the room seem larger than it is.

Combined with a huge window and vintage accents, quarry tile helps create the feeling that this bathroom is a natural extension of the porch beyond. Quarry tile should be sealed before being installed in locations that will be frequently exposed to water.

Installing a Tile Floor

Tile flooring should be durable and slip-resistant. Look for floor tile that is textured or soft-glazed—for slip resistance—and has a Class or Group rating of 3, 4, or 5—for strength. Floor tile should also be glazed for protection from staining. If you use unglazed tile, be sure to seal it properly after installation. See pages 11 through 35 for more information on selecting floor tile.

Standard grouts also need stain protection. Mix your grout with a latex additive, and apply a grout sealer after the new grout sets, then reapply the sealer once a year thereafter. Successful tile installation involves careful preparation of the floor and the proper combination of materials. For an underlayment, cementboard is the best for use over wood subfloors in bathrooms, since it is stable and undamaged by moisture (page 246). Thinset is the most common adhesive for floor tile. It comes as a dry powder that is mixed with water. Premixed organic adhesives generally are not recommended for floors.

If you want to install trim tiles, consider their placement as you plan the layout. Some base-trim tile is set on the floor, with its finished edge flush with the field tile; other types are installed on top of the field tile.

Tools & Materials ▸

Chalk line	Foam brush
¼" square-notched trowel	Tile
	Thinset mortar
Drill	Tile spacers
Rubber mallet	2 × 4
Tile-cutting tools	Threshold material
Needlenose pliers	Grout
Utility knife	Latex additive
Grout float	(mortar and grout)
Grout sponge	Grout sealer
Buff rag	Silicone caulk

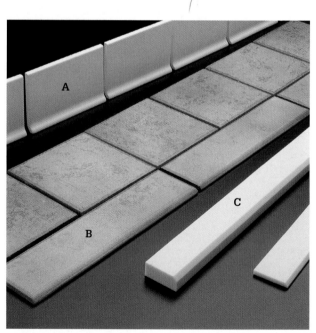

Trim and finishing materials for tile installations include base-trim tiles (A), which fit around the room perimeter, and bullnose tiles (B), used at doorways and other transition areas. Doorway thresholds (C) are made from synthetic materials as well as natural materials, such as marble, and come in thicknesses ranging from ¼" to ¾" to match different floor levels.

How to Install Cementboard Underlayment

1

Starting at the longest wall, spread thinset mortar on the subfloor in a figure-eight pattern. Spread only enough mortar for one sheet at a time. (See pages 260 to 261 for a full description of how to mix and apply thinset mortar.) Set the cementboard on the mortar with the rough side up, making sure the edges are offset from the subfloor seams.

2

Fasten cementboard to the subfloor, using 1½" cementboard screws. Drive the screw heads flush with the surface. Continue spreading mortar and installing sheets along the wall, leaving a ⅛" gap at all joints and a ¼" gap along the room perimeter. (See page 246 for full description of installing cementboard.)

Establishing Reference Lines for Floor Tile Installation ▸

To establish reference lines, position the first line (X) between the centerpoints of opposite sides of the room. Snap a chalk line between these points. Next, establish a second line perpendicular to the first. Snap a second reference line (Y) across the room.

Make sure the lines are exactly perpendicular, using the 3-4-5 triangle method. (For a full description of establishing perpendicular reference lines for floor projects, see page 41).

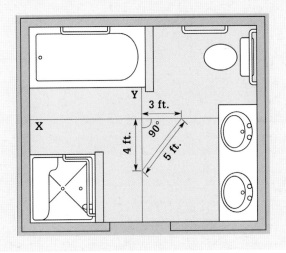

How to Install a Tile Floor

Draw reference lines and dry-fit full tiles along both lines, adjusting the layout as necessary. Mix a batch of thinset mortar (see pages 260 to 261), and spread it evenly against both reference lines of one quadrant. Use the notched edge of the trowel to create furrows in the mortar bed. *Note: For large or uneven tiles, you may need a trowel with ⅜" or larger notches.*

Set the first tile in the corner of the quadrant where the reference lines intersect. When setting tiles that are 8" square or larger, twist each tile slightly as you set it into position.

Using a soft rubber mallet, gently rap the central area of each tile a few times to set it evenly into the mortar.

Variation: For mosaic sheets, use a ³⁄₁₆" V-notched trowel to spread the mortar, and use a grout float to press the sheets into the mortar. Apply pressure gently to avoid creating an uneven surface.

To ensure consistent spacing between tiles, place plastic tile spacers at the corners of the set tile. *Note: With mosaic sheets, use spacers equal to the gaps between tiles.*

5

6

Set tiles into the mortar along the reference lines. Make sure the tiles fit neatly against the spacers. To make sure the tiles are level with one another, lay a straight piece of 2 × 4 across several tiles, and rap the board with a mallet. Lay tile in the remaining area covered with mortar. Repeat steps 1 through 5, working in small sections, until you reach walls or fixtures.

Measure and mark tiles for cutting to fit against walls and into corners, then cut the tiles to fit, following the tips on pages 254 to 259. Apply thinset mortar directly to the back of the cut tiles, instead of the floor, using the notched edge of the trowel to furrow the mortar. Set the tiles.

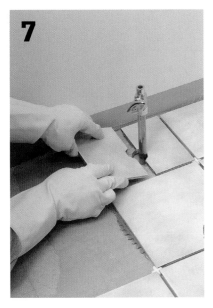

7

8

9

Measure, cut, and install tiles requiring notches or curves to fit around obstacles, such as exposed pipes or toilet drains.

Remove the spacers with needlenose pliers before the mortar hardens. Inspect the joints and remove high spots of mortar that could show through the grout, using a utility knife. Install tile in the remaining quadrants, completing one quadrant at a time.

Install threshold material in doorways. Set the threshold in thinset mortar so the top is even with the tile. Use the same spacing used for the tiles. Let the mortar cure for at least 24 hours.

(continued)

Mix a small batch of grout, following the manufacturer's directions. (For unglazed or stone tile, add a release agent to prevent the grout from bonding to the tile surfaces.) Starting in a corner, pour the grout over the tile. Spread the grout outward from the corner, pressing firmly on the grout float to completely fill the joints. For best results, tilt the float at a 60° angle to the floor and use a figure-eight motion.

Use the grout float to remove excess grout from the surface of the tile. Wipe diagonally across the joints, holding the float in a nearly vertical position. Continue applying grout and wiping off excess until about 25 sq. ft. of the floor has been grouted.

Remove excess grout by wiping a damp grout sponge diagonally over about 2 sq. ft. of the tile at a time. Rinse the sponge in cool water between wipes. Wipe each area only once; repeated wiping can pull grout from the joints. Repeat steps 10 through 12 to apply grout to the rest of the floor. Allow the grout to dry for about 4 hours, then use a soft cloth to buff the tile surface and remove any remaining grout film.

After the grout has cured completely (check the manufacturer's instructions), apply grout sealer to the grout lines, using a small sponge brush or sash brush. Avoid brushing sealer onto the tile surfaces. Wipe up any excess sealer immediately.

How to Install Base & Trim Tile

1

Dry-fit the trim tiles to determine the best spacing (grout lines in base tile do not always align with grout lines in the floor tile). Use rounded bullnose tiles at outside corners, and mark tiles for cutting as needed.

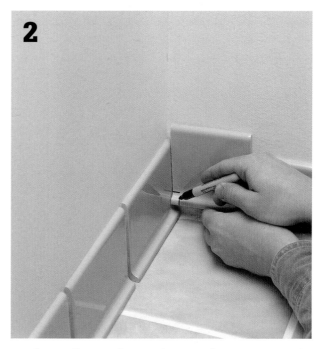

2

Leaving a ⅛" expansion gap between tiles at corners, mark any contour cuts necessary to allow the coved edges to fit together. Use a jigsaw with a tungsten carbide blade to make curved cuts.

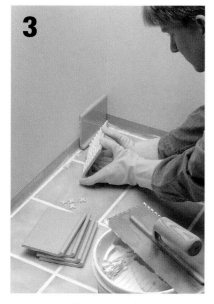

3

Begin installing base-trim tiles at an inside corner. Use a notched trowel to apply wall-tile adhesive to the back of each tile. Slip ⅛" spacers under the tiles to create an expansion joint. Set the tiles by pressing them firmly onto the wall.

4

At outside corners, use a double-bullnose tile on one side to cover the edge of the adjoining tile.

5

After the adhesive dries, grout the vertical joints between tiles, and apply grout along the tops of the tiles to make a continuous grout line. After the grout cures, fill the expansion joint at the bottom of the tiles with silicone caulk.

How to Set a Running Bond Tile Pattern

Start running bond tile by dry-fitting tile to establish working reference lines. Dry-fit a few tiles side by side using spacers. Measure the total width of the fitted section (A). Use this measurement to snap a series of equally spaced parallel lines to help keep your tiles straight during installation.

Starting at a point where the layout lines intersect, spread thinset mortar to a small section and lay the first row of tiles. Apply mortar directly to the underside of any tiles that extend outside the mortar bed. Offset the next row by a measurement that's equal to one-half the length of the tile and one-half the width of the grout line.

Continue setting tiles, filling one quadrant at a time. Use the parallel reference lines as guides to keep the rows straight. Immediately wipe away any mortar from the surface of the tiles. When finished, allow the mortar to cure, then grout and clean the tile (see page 60).

How to Set Hexagonal Tile

Snap perpendicular reference lines on the underlayment. Lay out three or four tiles in each direction along the layout lines. Place plastic spacers between the tiles to maintain even spacing. Measure the length of this layout in both directions (A and B). Use measurement A to snap a series of equally spaced parallel lines across the entire floor, then do the same for measurement B in the other direction.

Apply thinset mortar to small sections at a time and begin setting tile. Apply mortar directly to the underside of any tiles that extend outside the mortar bed. Continue setting the tiles, using the grid layout and spacers to keep the tiles aligned. Wipe off any mortar from the tile surface. When finished, allow the mortar to set, then grout.

How to Set a Diagonal Pattern within a Border

Plan your border layout in the room (see pages 38 to 44). Dry-fit border tiles with spacers in the planned area. Make sure the border tiles are aligned with the reference lines. Dry-fit tiles at the outside corners of the border arrangement. Adjust the tile positions as necessary to create a layout with minimal cutting. When the layout of the tiles is set, snap chalk lines around the border tiles and trace along the edges of the outside tiles. Install the border tiles.

Draw diagonal layout lines at a 45° angle to the perpendicular reference lines.

Use standard tile-setting techniques to set field tiles inside the border. Kneel on a wide board to distribute your weight if you need to work in a tiled area that has not cured overnight.

Installing a Stone & Mosaic Tile Floor

The project that follows combines 4 × 4" tumbled stone with a stone mosaic medallion and border to produce a decorative effect in an entryway. This idea could be adapted for many rooms. You could border a seating area or create the effect of a rug in front of a fireplace, for example. To lay out a similar design, refer to pages 43 and 44, then center the medallion within the border.

The techniques for setting natural stone are virtually the same ones used with ceramic tile. There are several special considerations, however.

First, stone tile cracks more easily than ceramic. It's extremely important to provide a firm, flat substrate for stone tile projects, especially when you're using large tiles. The larger the tile, the more susceptible it is to stress fractures if the floor structure doesn't support it adequately. See pages 228 to 231 for more information on repairing and strengthening subfloors; see pages 232 to 235 for information on installing underlayment.

Natural stone is subject to greater variation from one tile to the next than manufactured materials. Cartons of some stone tile, especially larger polished stone varieties, may include warped tiles. Be sure to buy enough tile that any severely warped tiles can be sorted out and returned.

Some stone should be sealed before it's set because grout tends to stain it. Ask your dealer for specific recommendations.

Tools & Materials ▸

Chalk line	Mosaic tile
¼" square-notched trowel	Mosaic medallion
	Thinset mortar
Rubber mallet	Tile spacers
Tile-cutting tools	2 × 4 lumber
Needlenose pliers	Threshold material
Utility knife	Grout
Grout float	Latex additive
Grout sponge	(mortar and grout)
Buff rag	Grout sealer
Foam brush	Silicone caulk
4 × 4" stone tile	

Tips for Setting Stone Tile Floors ▸

Make sure the subfloor is flat and firm. If problems exist, resolve them before beginning the tile project (see pages 228 to 231). This is important for any stone tile floor but critical for a polished stone tile floor.

Check for warped tiles. Lay polished stone tiles next to one another and check carefully. Mark tiles that are slightly warped and build up thinset mortar to level them during installation. Return significantly warped tile to the dealer.

Dry-lay polished stone tile floors, with 1/16" spacers. (Plan to use unsanded grout.) Use larger spacers (and sanded grout) for informal stone floors.

Use white thinset mortar for light-colored marble, travertine, and other natural stones, which are somewhat translucent. Take extra care to create a very even surface when combing the mortar.

Seal tiles before installation to help keep contrasting grout from staining the stone. Check manufacturer's recommendations or consult your tile retailer for suggestions. This is particularly important when dealing with porous or rough-surfaced stone.

Keep grout from staining stone tile by wiping the tiles early and often, using a clean, damp cloth.

How to Set a Stone & Mosaic Tile Floor

Measure the area and make a scaled diagram of the space. Measure the mosaic medallion and determine the size and placement of the bordered area (see pages 38 through 44 for details).

Install and tape cementboard in the project area. (See pages 246 to 247 for full details.)

Snap perpendicular reference lines. Check the lines for squareness, using the "3-4-5 triangle" method (see page 39 for further information).

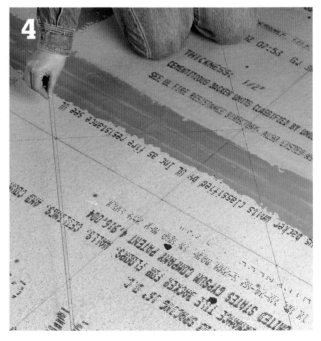

On each line, mark a point equally distant from the center. If your mosaic medallion is a 12" square, mark the points at 12"; if it's a 24" square, mark the points at 24", and so on. Snap chalk lines to connect the points, establishing lines at a 45° angle.

Following the layout created in step 1, measure and mark placement lines for the border. (Make sure these lines are aligned with the first set of reference lines.) Cut mosaic tiles into strips and dry-fit the border.

Dry-fit the tiles at the outside corners of the border arrangement, aligning the tile with the diagonal reference lines. Use spacers and adjust as necessary. When the layout of the tiles is set, trace the edges of the outside tiles.

Set the field tile, cutting tile as necessary (see pages 56 to 63 for full details on setting tile). Remove the spacers. Let the mortar cure according to manufacturer's instructions. Set the border tile.

Place the medallion in the center of the bordered area, aligning it with the diagonal reference lines. Dry-fit the field tiles within the border, using spacers and aligning the tile with the perpendicular reference lines.

(continued)

9

For tricky cuts, make paper templates to match the tile size. Later, use the templates to mark tiles for cutting.

10

Determine placement of accent tiles within field tile. Measure the field accent tile and mark cutting lines on field tile to accommodate them.

11

Set medallion, then the field tile within the border. (Again, avoid placing your weight on newly set tiles.) Remove the spacers and let the mortar dry overnight or according to manufacturer's instructions.

Tip ▶

If it is absolutely necessary to work from newly set tile, kneel on a wide board to distribute your weight.

12

Install **threshold material** in doorways. Set the threshold in thinset mortar so the top is even with the tile. Use the same spacing used for the tiles. Let the mortar cure for at least 24 hours.

13

Prepare a small batch of grout and fill the tile joints (see page 60 for details on grouting tile). When the grout has cured, seal the grout lines, using a small sponge brush or sash brush.

14

Add **wood baseboards** or base-trim tiles at the edges of the room.

Installing a Glass Mosaic Floor

Throughout history, mosaic tile has been more than a floor or wall covering—it's been an art form. In fact, the Latin origins of the word mosaic refer to art "worthy of the muses." Mosaic tile is beautiful and durable, and working with it is easier than ever today. Modern mosaic floor tile is available in squares that are held together by an underlayer of fabric mesh. These squares are set in much the same way as larger tile, but their flexibility makes them slightly more difficult to hold, place, and move. The instructions given with this project simplify the handling of these squares.

Some manufacturers stabilize mosaic squares with a paper facing on the front of the square. Most facings of this type can be removed with warm water, which we describe here. However, this can vary, so be sure to read and follow manufacturer's recommendations regarding this facing and its removal.

The colors of mosaic tile shift just as much as any other tile, so make sure all the boxes you buy are from the same lot and batch. Colors often vary from one box to another, too, but mixing tile from boxes makes any shifts less noticeable.

It's also important to know that adhesive made for other tile may not work with glass or specialty mosaic tile. Consult your tile retailer for advice on the right mortar or mastic for your project. Before you start, clean and prepare the floor (see pages 218 through 227). Measure the room and draw reference lines (page 41). Lay out sheets of tile along both the vertical and horizontal reference lines. If these lines will produce small or difficult cuts at the edges, shift them until you're satisfied with the layout.

Tools & Materials ▸

Tape measure	Mosaic tile
Chalk line	Tile adhesive
¼" notched trowel	Tile spacers
Grout float	Grout
Grout sponge	Latex additive
Buff rag	Grout sealer
Sponge applicator	Tile clippers
Needlenose pliers	2 × 4

How to Install a Glass Mosaic Floor

Beginning at the intersection of the horizontal and vertical lines, apply the recommended adhesive in one quadrant. Spread it outward evenly with a notched trowel. Lay down only as much adhesive as you can cover in 10 to 15 minutes.

Stabilize a sheet of tile by randomly inserting three or four plastic spacers into the open joints.

Pick up diagonally opposite corners of the square and move it to the intersection of the horizontal and vertical references lines. Align the sides with the reference lines and gently press one corner into place on the adhesive. Slowly lower the opposite corner, making sure the sides remain square with the reference lines. Massage the sheet into the adhesive, being careful not to press too hard or twist the sheet out of position. Continue setting tile, filling in one square area after another.

(continued)

When two or three sheets are in place, lay a scrap of 2 × 4 wrapped in carpet across them and tap it with a rubber mallet to set the fabric mesh into the adhesive and force out any trapped air.

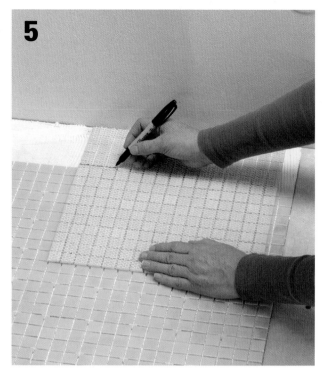

When you've tiled up close to the wall or another boundary, lay a full mosaic sheet into position and mark it for trimming. If you've planned well and are installing small-tile mosaics, you can often avoid the need to cut tiles.

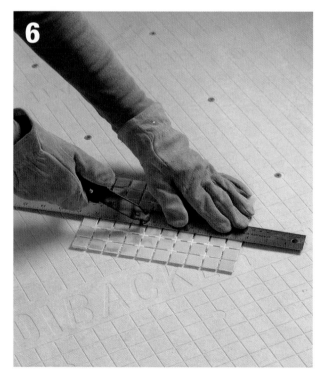

If you do need to cut tiles in the mosaic sheet, and not just the backing, score the tiles with a tile cutter. Be sure the tiles are still attached to the backing. Add spacers between the individual tiles to prevent them from shifting as you score.

After you've scored the tiles, cut them each individually with a pair of tile nippers.

8

Set tile in the remaining quadrants. Let the adhesive cure according to the manufacturer's instructions. Remove spacers with a needlenose pliers. Mix a batch of grout and fill the joints (see page 60). Allow the grout to dry, according to manufacturer's instructions.

9

Mosaic tile has a much higher ratio of grout to tile than larger tiles do, so it is especially important to seal the grout with a quality sealer after it has cured.

Working Around Obstacles ▸

1

To work around pipes and other obstructions, cut through the backing to create an access point for the sheet. Then, remove the tiles within the mosaic sheet to clear a space large enough for the pipe or other obstruction.

2

Set the cut sheet into an adhesive bed, and then cut small pieces of tile and fit them into the layout as necessary.

Installing an Original Mosaic Design

In olden days, a mosaic was created slowly and painstakingly by an artist. Some still create mosaics this way, but today you don't have to be an accomplished artist to make your own tile mosaic. With the help of technology and the right supplies, practically anyone can create and set an original mosaic.

You can create a mosaic pattern with colored pencils and graph paper, or you can use a digital image and a color printer. Basic desktop publishing programs, and even some word processing programs, allow you to size and crop an image, overlay a scaled grid, and print it out. Or, you can actually build an electronic grid of photo boxes and assign a color to each box individually as a layout reference. If you'd rather not take such a hands-on approach to creating your own pattern, there are several websites on the Internet that can adapt any image you send them to a mosaic pattern for a nominal charge.

The appearance of your final project depends largely on available sizes and colors at the mosaic tile supplies retailer. When making your tile purchase, add at least 10 percent for cutting and breakage.

Tools & Materials ▸

Computer and printer
Chalk line
¼" notched trowel
Rubber mallet
Tile-cutting tools
Needlenose pliers
Utility knife
Grout float
Grout sponge
Buff rag
Foam brush
⅜" transparent graph paper
⅜" mosaic floor tiles
Mosaic mounting media
Tile grids
Photograph or other image
Floor tile
Thinset mortar
Latex additive (mortar and grout)
Grout sealer

How to Install an Original Mosaic Design

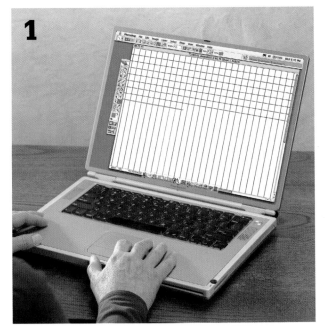

Browse through some images for ideas and inspiration, focusing especially on simple, geometric forms. Choose a tile size (we used ¾ × ¾") and create a scaled grid that represents the whole project layout. You can use a computer program to do this, or draw your own grid, or even use graph paper.

Using your reference images as a general guide, fill in the boxes with color to replicate the pattern you like. Because this involves a lot of trial and error to get the best results, you're much better off using the computer program for this part.

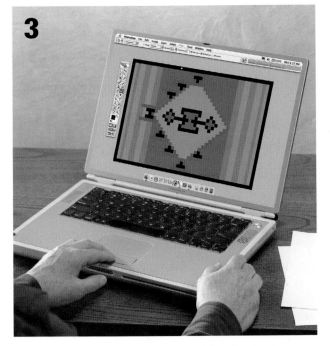

Leave a couple of squares all around for a border. Once you've arrived at the pattern you like, add the border. Borders can be a solid color or multi-colored, but they should contrast with the adjoining tiles if possible.

Print the pattern on a color printer. Lay it on the floor and view it from several angles—you may find that it looks very different than it did on the computer. Make any adjustments you feel improves the pattern.

(continued)

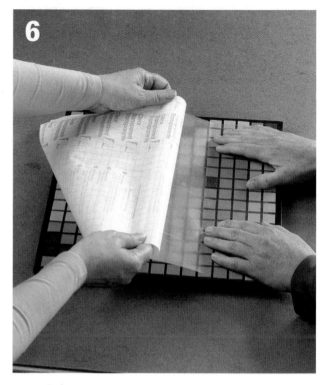

Using the pattern as a guide, assemble the mosaics into the tile grids. Start at the intersection of the horizontal and vertical reference lines and mark off each square on the printout as the corresponding square is filled in the grid.

As each frame is completed, cover it with mosaic mounting media. Peel the backing off the media and press it over the tile grid. Rub the media to make sure it sticks to each tile. (This may be easier with a helper.)

Hold the mounting media at the corners, and lift the tile from the grid. (Handle the media carefully to make sure the tile stays in place.) Set the section aside.

Remove any old flooring and prepare the floor (see page 218 through 227). Measure the area and snap reference lines (page 41).

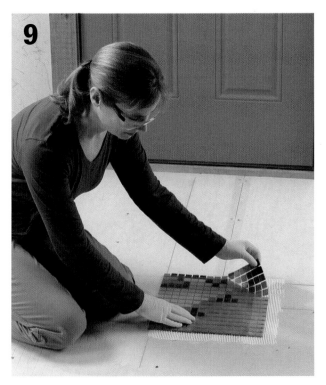

9

Spread thinset mortar in a grid-sized section at the intersection of the horizontal and vertical reference lines. Position the mosaic at the exact intersection of the lines and press it into position.

10

Use a grout float to seat the tile in the mortar. Slide the grout float over the surface of the mounting media, pressing down gently.

11

Reach under the mounting media to set a spacer at each corner of the section and one in the middle of each side.

12

Continue filling tile grids and adding them to the mosaic in an orderly fashion.

(continued)

Allow the mortar to cure, according to manufacturer's instructions. When the mortar is dry, carefully peel the mounting media away from each section of tile.

Dry-lay the field tile around the custom mosaic, and cut tiles as necessary. Then apply thinset mortar in small sections and place field tile until the entire floor is tiled.

Mix a batch of grout, and spread it over the tile and press it into the joints, using a grout float (see page 60).

Wipe away excess grout with a damp sponge. Continue gently wiping the surface until it's as clear as possible. Rinse the sponge frequently and change the water as necessary. Allow the area to dry. Polish off remaining grout residue with a clean, dry cloth.

More Ideas for Mosaics ▸

As mosaic designs have moved into the mainstream, more and more ways of creating them have become available and more and more materials are being incorporated into them. Consider the following options.

To use computer programs to generate your design, you need a computer and the specialized software program, access to a scanner, and a photograph or piece of artwork to scan. After you import the image file, the program reads the file, assigns tile colors to it, and creates a pattern—some even produce a precise shopping list for the project. The process is fairly easy and the results can be spectacular. Following a computer generated chart, you place tiles in grids and use mosaic mounting media to transfer them to the project area (see pages 75 through 78).

Many mosaic retailers or online supply services offer design information or templates if you buy your supplies from them. Some offer everything from simple color gradations to exquisite designs—and the design shown here shows just how stunning a simple color gradation can be. You provide an idea or image and they take it from there, producing a shopping list and directions for completing the mosaic. Search online or ask your favorite mosaic retailer if they offer this service.

Cross-stitch and needlepoint patterns are designed to create lovely patterns from small squares of color. Simpler patterns can be used as mosaic designs, too. Assign tile colors for the various thread colors indicated on the pattern. Set the tile as described on page 75.

Building a Tiled Shower Base

Building a custom-tiled shower base lets you choose the shape and size of your shower rather than having its dimensions dictated by available products. Building the base is quite simple, though it does require time and some knowledge of basic masonry techniques because the base is formed primarily using mortar. What you get for your time and trouble can be spectacular.

Before designing a shower base, contact your local building department regarding code restrictions and to secure the necessary permits. Most codes require water controls to be accessible from outside the shower and describe acceptable door positions and operation. Requirements like these influence the size and position of the base.

Choosing the tile before finalizing the design lets you size the base to require mostly full tile. Showers are among the most frequently used amenities in the average home, so it really makes sense to build one that is comfortable and pleasing to your senses. Consider using small tile and gradate the color from top to bottom or in a sweep across the walls. Or, use trim tile and listellos on the walls to create an interesting focal point.

Whatever tile you choose, remember to seal the grout in your new shower and to maintain it carefully over the years. Full, water-resistant grout protects the structure of the shower and prolongs its useful life.

Tools & Materials ▶

Tape measure	3-piece shower drain
Circular saw	PVC primer
Hammer	PVC cement
Utility knife	Galvanized finish nails
Stapler	Galvanized metal lath
2-ft. level	Thick-bed floor mortar
Mortar mixing box	("deck mud")
Trowel	Latex mortar additive
Wood float	Laminating adhesive
Felt-tip marker	CPE waterproof
Ratchet wrench	membrane &
Expandable stopper	preformed dam
Drill	corners
Tin snips	CPE membrane
Torpedo level	solvent glue
Tools for installing tile	CPE membrane
(page 56)	sealant
2 × 4 and 2 × 10	Cementboard
framing lumber	and materials
16d galvanized	for installing
common nails	cementboard
15# building paper	Materials for
Staples	installing tile

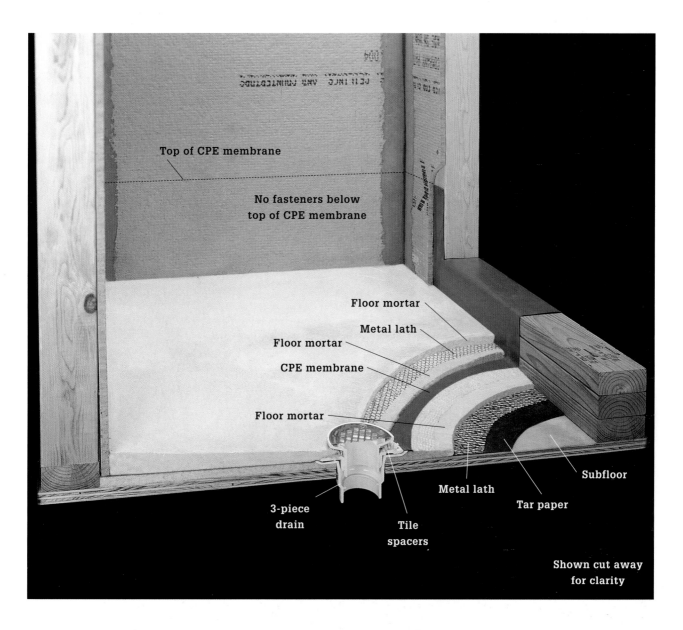

Top of CPE membrane

No fasteners below
top of CPE membrane

Floor mortar

Metal lath

Floor mortar

CPE membrane

Floor mortar

Subfloor

Metal lath

Tar paper

3-piece
drain

Tile
spacers

Shown cut away
for clarity

Tips for Building a Custom Shower Base ▸

A custom-tiled shower base is built in three layers to ensure proper water drainage: the pre pan, the shower pan, and the shower floor. A mortar pre pan is first built on top of the subfloor, establishing a slope toward the drain of ¼" for every 12" of shower floor. Next, a waterproof chlorinated polyethylene (CPE) membrane forms the shower pan, providing a watertight seal for the shower base. Finally, a second mortar bed reinforced with wire mesh is installed for the shower floor, providing a surface for tile installation. If water penetrates the tiled shower floor, the shower pan and sloped pre pan will direct it to the weep holes of the 3-piece drain.

One of the most important steps in building a custom-tiled shower base is testing the shower pan after installation (step 13). This allows you to locate and fix any leaks to prevent costly damage.

How to Build a Custom-tiled Shower Base

Remove building materials to expose subfloor and stud walls (see pages 222 through 227). Cut three 2 × 4s for the curb and fasten them to the floor joists and the studs at the shower threshold with 16d galvanized common nails. Also cut 2 × 10 lumber to size and install in the stud bays around the perimeter of the shower base.

Staple 15# building paper to the subfloor of the shower base. Disassemble the 3-piece shower drain and glue the bottom piece to the drain pipe with PVC cement. Partially screw the drain bolts into the drain piece, and stuff a rag into the drain pipe to prevent mortar from falling into the drain.

Mark the height of the bottom drain piece on the wall farthest from the center of the drain. Measure from the center of the drain straight across to that wall, then raise the height mark ¼" for every 12" of shower floor to slope the pre pan toward the drain. Trace a reference line at the height mark around the perimeter of the entire alcove, using a level.

Staple galvanized metal lath over the building paper; cut a hole in the lath ½" from the drain. Mix floor mortar (or "deck mud") to a fairly dry consistency, using a latex additive for strength; mortar should hold its shape when squeezed (inset). Trowel the mortar onto the subfloor, building the pre pan from the flange of the drain piece to the height line on the perimeter of the walls.

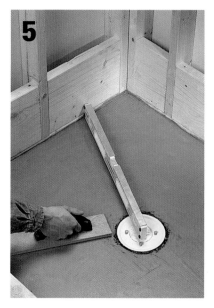

Continue using the trowel to form the pre pan, checking the slope using a level and filling any low spots with mortar. Finish the surface of the pre pan with a wood float until it is even and smooth. Allow the mortar to cure overnight.

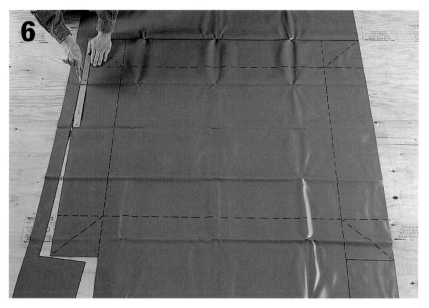

Measure the dimensions of the shower floor, and mark it out on a sheet of CPE waterproof membrane, using a felt-tipped marker. From the floor outline, measure out and mark an additional 8" for each wall and 16" for the curb end. Cut the membrane to size, using a utility knife and straightedge. Be careful to cut on a clean, smooth surface to prevent puncturing the membrane. Lay the membrane onto the shower pan.

Measure to find the exact location of the drain and mark it on the membrane, outlining the outer diameter of the drain flange. Cut a circular piece of CPE membrane roughly 2" larger than the drain flange, then use CPE membrane solvent glue to weld it into place and reinforce the seal at the drain.

Apply CPE sealant around the drain. Fold the membrane along the floor outline. Set the membrane over the pre pan so the reinforced drain seal is centered over the drain bolts. Working from the drain to the walls, carefully tuck the membrane tight into each corner, folding the extra material into triangular flaps.

(continued)

9

Apply CPE solvent glue to one side, press the flap flat, then staple it in place. Staple only the top edge of the membrane to the blocking; do not staple below the top of the curb, or on the curb itself.

10

At the shower curb, cut the membrane along the studs so it can be folded over the curb. Solvent-glue a dam corner at each inside corner of the curb. Do not fasten the dam corners with staples.

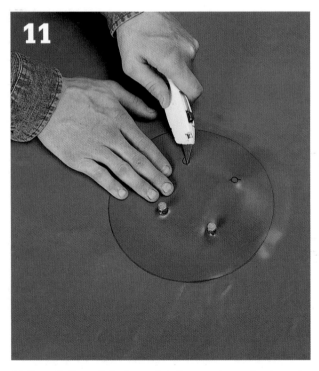

11

At the reinforced drain seal on the membrane, locate and mark the drain bolts. Press the membrane down around the bolts, then use a utility knife to carefully cut a slit just large enough for the bolts to poke through. Push the membrane down over the bolts.

12

Use a utility knife to carefully cut away only enough of the membrane to expose the drain and allow the middle drain piece to fit in place. Remove the drain bolts, then position the middle drain piece over the bolt holes. Reinstall the bolts, tightening them evenly and firmly to create a watertight seal.

Test the shower pan for leaks overnight. Place a balloon tester in the drain below the weep holes, and fill the pan with water, to 1" below the top of the curb. Mark the water level and let the water sit overnight. If the water level remains the same, the pan holds water. If the level is lower, locate and fix leaks in the pan using patches of membrane and CPE solvent.

Install cementboard on the alcove walls, using ¼" wood shims to lift the bottom edge off the CPE membrane. To prevent puncturing the membrane, do not use fasteners in the lower 8" of the cementboard. Cut a piece of metal lath to fit around the three sides of the curb. Bend the lath so it tightly conforms to the curb. Pressing the lath against the top of the curb, staple it to the outside face of the curb. Mix enough mortar for the two sides of the curb.

Overhang the front edge of the curb with a straight 1× board, so it is flush with the outer wall material. Apply mortar to the mesh with a trowel, building to the edge of the board. Clear away excess mortar, then use a torpedo level to check for plumb, making adjustments as needed. Repeat for the inside face of the curb. *Note: The top of the curb will be finished after tile is installed (step 19). Allow the mortar to cure overnight.*

Attach the drain strainer piece to the drain, adjusting it to a minimum of 1½" above the shower pan. On one wall, mark 1½" up from the shower pan, then use a level to draw a reference line around the perimeter of the shower base. Because the pre pan establishes the ¼" per foot slope, this measurement will maintain that slope.

(continued)

17

Spread tile spacers over the weep holes of the drain to prevent mortar from plugging the holes. Mix the floor mortar, then build up the shower floor to roughly half the thickness of the base. Cut metal lath to cover the mortar bed, keeping it ½" from the drain (see photo in step 18).

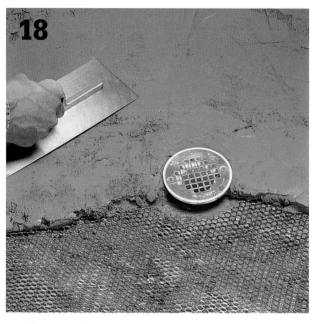

18

Continue to add mortar, building the floor to the reference line on the walls. Use a level to check the slope, and pack mortar into low spots with a trowel. Leave space at the drain for the thickness of the tile. Float the surface using a wood float until it is smooth and slopes evenly to the drain. When finished, allow the mortar to cure overnight before installing the tiles.

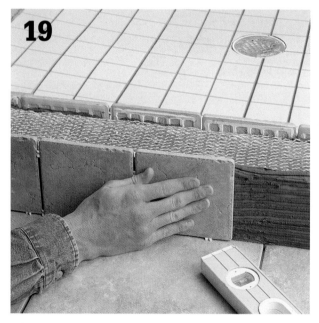

19

After the floor has cured, draw reference lines and establish the tile layout, then mix a batch of thinset mortar and install the floor tile (pages 56 to 63). At the curb, cut the tiles for the inside to protrude ½" above the unfinished top of the curb, and the tiles for the outside to protrude ⅝" above the top, establishing a ⅛" slope so water drains back into the shower. Use a level to check the tops of the tiles for level as you work.

20

Mix enough floor mortar to cover the unfinished top of the curb, then pack it in place between the tiles, using a trowel. Screed off the excess mortar flush with the tops of the side tiles. Allow the mortar to cure, then install bullnose cap tile. Install the wall tile, then grout, clean, and seal all the tile (page 60). After the grout has cured fully, run a bead of silicone caulk around all inside corners to create control joints.

Textured surfaces improve the safety of tile floors, especially in wet areas such as this open shower. The shower area is designated effectively by a simple shift in color and size.

The raised curb on this open shower keeps most of the water headed toward the drain. But no matter, the entire bathroom is tiled, so stray droplets are no problem.

Mosaic tile, with its mesh backing and small shapes, often works well on curved walls such as the one that forms this shower. The rectangular shape of the individual mosaic tiles complements the shape of the post at the corner of the shower.

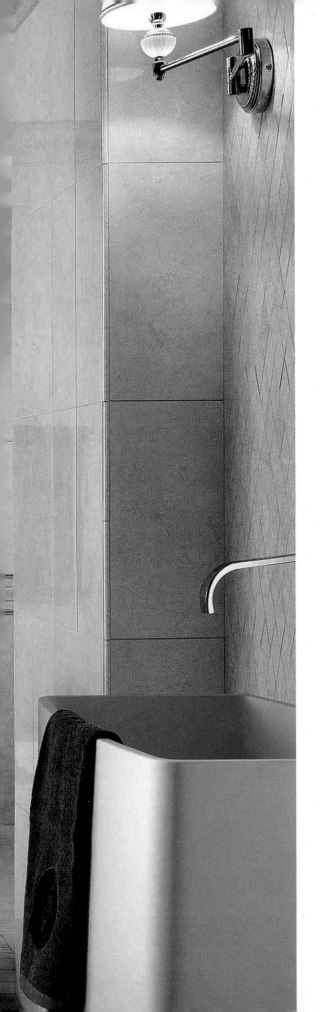

Wall Projects

This chapter starts with a very basic wall project that's practically one-size-fits-all. Then, we show you how to tile a tub alcove, another tile project that's frequently undertaken by do-it-yourselfers.

From those beginnings, it's a small step to embellishing an existing tile wall with a medallion or decorative tile, or tiling a fireplace surround or kitchen backsplash. With the confidence developed in those projects, you'll be ready to tile a tub deck or build a wall niche, if the opportunity arises.

The projects in this chapter introduce you to several new and interesting techniques. The tub deck project shows you how to set several types of trim tile and the wall niche project illustrates how to set irregular-shaped, groutless tile. The medallion project walks you through embellishing an otherwise plain tiled wall without simply starting over.

Use these projects as jumping off points, as places from which to let your imagination soar. Study the techniques and information presented here, then throw in some accent tiles, add splashes of color—whatever it takes to make a project your own.

In This Chapter:

- Installing a Tile Wall
- Tiling a Fireplace Surround
- Tiling a Kitchen Backsplash
- Building a Tiled Wall Niche
- Embellishing a Tiled Wall
- Building a Tiled Tub Deck

Striking color combinations are made possible by the natural variations in stone.

Mosaic tile can be used to create elaborate designs like this shower.

Handpainted tiles set together make a striking statement on an otherwise plain wall.

Mosaic tile can also be used to create simple combinations that allow the beauty of the materials to take center stage.

Tile defines a hearth area and fireplace surround, and merges them into this tranquil setting.

This mantel and fireplace surround rely on shape and size for effect, subtly blending into the floor without stealing too much attention from its distinctive pattern.

Mitering the corners adds special interest to ledges and countertops.

Called "subway tile," tiles in this size and shape are often set with the joints offset rather than aligned. This attractive pattern isn't difficult, but does require more careful planning than a traditional set.

This large contemporary bathroom is broken into distinct functional areas by the tile. The doorless shower is defined by field tile in a straight set, while the dressing area is marked by a border and the reversal of color between the field and the edges. The mirror above the sink is framed by field tile set on the diagonal. Finally, the sink area is set off by a shift in the size and shape of the field tile.

Although the wall is set with a combination of similar tiles, liners and listellos mark the transition from a straight to a diagonal set. This breaks up what would otherwise be a broad—and possibly boring—expanse of plain tile.

Combinations of trim tile, such as chair rail, listellos, and baseboard contribute shape, texture, and definition to walls.

They require careful planning, but stunning effects can be achieved through color banding and variations in setting patterns. On the wall at the far right in this bathroom, border tile and liners sparkle against white tile. On the wall at left, liners frame the mirror, which is set within a frame of white and decorative tile. Framed by liners and a diagonal set, the sink becomes a decorative element for the room.

Installing a Tile Wall

Tile is an ideal covering for walls in kitchens and bathrooms, but there's no reason to limit its use to those rooms. It's not as common in North American homes, but in Europe tile has been used in rooms throughout the house for generations. And why not? Beautiful, practical, easy to clean and maintain, tile walls are well suited to many spaces. On the preceding pages, you've seen some design ideas for tile walls. Now it's time to get down to business.

When shopping for tile, keep in mind that tiles that are at least 6" × 6" are easier to install than small tiles, because they require less cutting and cover more surface area. Larger tiles also have fewer grout lines that must be cleaned and maintained. Check out the selection of trim and specialty tiles and ceramic accessories that are available to help you customize your project. (See pages 11 through 35 for information on selecting tile.)

Most wall tile is designed to have narrow grout lines (less than 1/8" wide) filled with unsanded grout. Grout lines wider than 1/8" should be filled with sanded floor-tile grout. Either type will last longer if it contains, or is mixed with, a latex additive. To prevent staining, it's a good idea to seal your grout after it fully cures, then once a year thereafter.

You can use standard drywall or water-resistant drywall (called "greenboard") as a backer for walls in dry areas. In wet areas, install tile over cementboard.

Made from cement and fiberglass, cementboard cannot be damaged by water, though moisture can pass through it. To protect the framing, install a waterproof membrane, such as roofing felt or polyethylene sheeting, between the framing members and the cementboard. Be sure to tape and finish the seams between cementboard panels before laying the tile.

See page 45 for information on planning and laying out tile walls.

Tools & Materials ▸

Tile-cutting tools	Dry-set tile mortar
Marker	with latex additive
Tape measure	Ceramic wall tile
4-ft. level	Ceramic trim tile
Notched trowel	(as needed)
Mallet	2 × 4
Grout float	Carpet scrap
Grout sponge	Tile grout with latex
Soft cloth	additive
Small paintbrush	Tub & tile caulk
or foam brush	Alkaline grout sealer
Caulk gun	Cardboard
Straight 1 × 2	Story stick/pole

How to Set Wall Tile

Design the layout and mark the reference lines (see pages 39 to 42). Begin installation with the second row of tiles above the floor. If the layout requires cut tiles for this row, mark and cut the tiles for the entire row at one time.

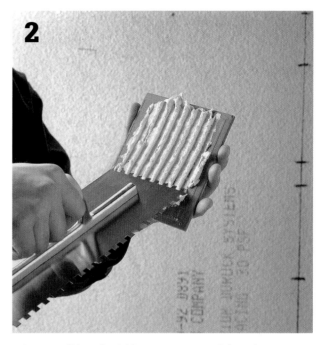

Mix a small batch of thinset mortar containing a latex additive. (Some mortar has additive mixed in by the manufacturer and some must have additive mixed in separately.) Cover the back of the first tile with adhesive, using a ¼" notched trowel.

Variation: Spread adhesive on a small section of the wall, then set the tiles into the adhesive. Thinset adhesive sets quickly, so work quickly if you choose this installation method.

Beginning near the center of the wall, apply the tile to the wall with a slight twisting motion, aligning it exactly with the horizontal and vertical reference lines. When placing cut tiles, position the cut edges where they will be least visible.

(continued)

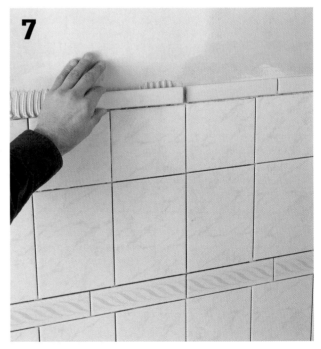

Continue installing tiles, working from the center to the sides in a pyramid pattern. Keep the tiles aligned with the reference lines. If the tiles are not self-spacing, use plastic spacers inserted in the corner joints to maintain even grout lines. The base row should be the last row of full tiles installed. Cut tile as necessary (see pages 254 to 259).

As small sections of tile are completed, "set" the tile by laying a scrap of 2 × 4 wrapped with carpet onto the tile and rapping it lightly with a mallet. This embeds the tile solidly in the adhesive and creates a flat, even surface.

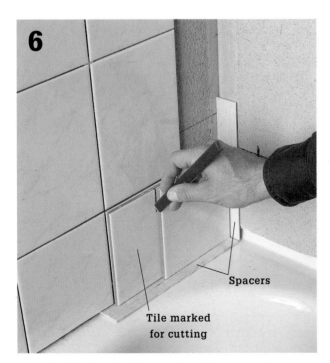

Spacers

Tile marked for cutting

To mark tiles for straight cuts, begin by taping ⅛" spacers against the surfaces below and to the side of the tile. Position a tile directly over the last full tile installed, then place a third tile so the edge butts against the spacers. Trace the edge of the top tile onto the middle tile to mark it for cutting.

Install any trim tiles, such as the bullnose edge tiles shown above, at border areas. Wipe away excess mortar along the top edges of the edge tiles. Use bullnose and corner bullnose (with two adjacent bullnose edges) tiles at outside corners to cover the rough edges of the adjoining tiles.

8

Let mortar dry completely (12 to 24 hours), then mix a batch of grout containing latex additive. Apply the grout with a rubber grout float, using a sweeping motion to force it deep into the joints. Do not grout joints adjoining bathtubs, floors, or room corners. These will serve as expansion joints and will be caulked later.

9

Wipe a damp grout sponge diagonally over the tile, rinsing the sponge in cool water between wipes. Wipe each area only once; repeated wiping can pull grout from the joints. Allow the grout to dry for about 4 hours, then use a soft cloth to buff the tile surface and remove any remaining grout film.

10

When the grout has cured completely, use a small foam brush to apply grout sealer to the joints, following the manufacturer's directions. Avoid brushing sealer on the tile surfaces, and wipe up excess sealer immediately.

11

Seal expansion joints at the floor and corners with silicone caulk. After the caulk dries, buff the tile with a dry, soft cloth.

How to Install Wall Tile in a Bathtub Alcove

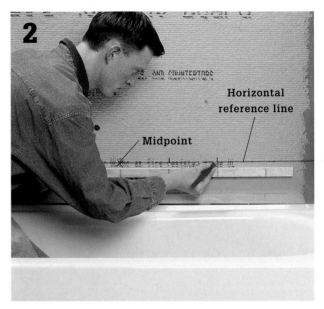

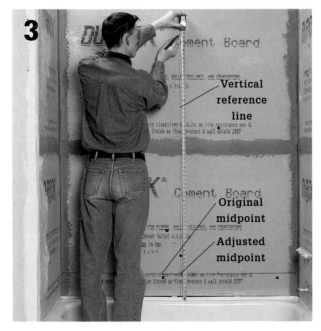

Beginning with the back wall, measure up and mark a point at a distance equal to the height of one ceramic tile (if the tub edge is not level, measure up from the lowest spot). Draw a level line through this point, along the entire back wall. This line represents a tile grout line and will be used as a reference line for making the entire tile layout.

Measure and mark the midpoint on the horizontal reference line. Using a story stick, mark along the reference line where the vertical grout joints will be located. If the story stick shows that the corner tiles will be less than half of a full tile width, move the midpoint half the width of a tile in either direction and mark (shown in next step).

Use a level to draw a vertical reference line through the adjusted midpoint from the tub edge to the ceiling. Measure up from the tub edge along the vertical reference line and mark the rough height of the top row of tiles.

Use the story stick to mark the horizontal grout joints along the vertical reference line, beginning at the mark for the top row of tiles. If the cut tiles at the tub edge will be less than half the height of a full tile, move the top row up half the height of a tile. *Note: If tiling to a ceiling, evenly divide the tiles to be cut at the ceiling and tub edge, as for the corner tiles.*

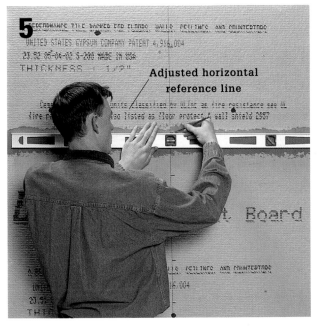

Use a level to draw an adjusted horizontal reference line through the vertical reference line at a grout joint mark close to the center of the layout. This splits the tile area into four workable quadrants.

Use a level to transfer the adjusted horizontal reference line from the back wall to both side walls, then follow step 3 through step 6 to lay out both side walls. Adjust the layout as needed so the final column of tiles ends at the outside edge of the tub. Use only the adjusted horizontal and vertical reference lines for ceramic tile installation.

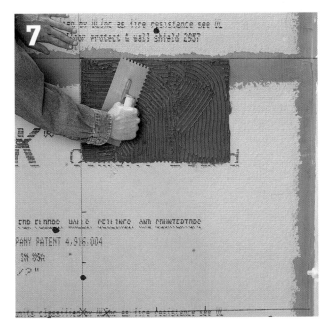

Mix a small batch of thinset mortar containing a latex additive. (Some mortar has additive mixed in by the manufacturer and some must have additive mixed separately.) Spread adhesive on a small section of the wall, along both legs of one quadrant, using a ¼" notched trowel.

Use the edge of the trowel to create furrows in the mortar. Set the first tile in the corner of the quadrant where the lines intersect, using a slight twisting motion. Align the tile exactly with both reference lines. When placing cut tiles, position the cut edges where they will be least visible.

(continued)

Continue installing tiles, working from the center out into the field of the quadrant. Keep the tiles aligned with the reference lines and tile in one quadrant at a time. If the tiles are not self-spacing, use plastic spacers inserted in the corner joints to maintain even grout lines (inset). The base row against the tub edge should be the last row of tiles installed.

Install trim tiles, such as the bullnose tiles shown above, at border areas. Wipe away excess mortar along the top edges of the edge tiles.

Mark and cut tiles to fit around all plumbing accessories or plumbing fixtures. Refer to pages 254 to 259 for tile cutting techniques.

Install any ceramic accessories by applying thinset mortar to the back side, then pressing the accessory into place. Use masking tape to support the weight until the mortar dries (inset). Fill the tub with water, then seal expansion joints around the bathtub, floor, and corners with silicone caulk (see page 201).

Variation: Tiling Bathroom Walls

Layout adjusted so the row of accent tiles is unbroken by medicine cabinet.

Tiles at each end of the same wall should be cut to a similar size.

Row of trimmed tiles should be positioned near the top and bottom of tiled area to make them less obvious.

Tiles above tub should be full size or nearly full size.

Tiling an entire bathroom requires careful planning. The bathroom shown here was designed so that the tiles directly above the bathtub (the most visible surface) are nearly full height. To accomplish this, cut tiles were used in the second row up from the floor. The short second row also allows the row of accent tiles to run uninterrupted below the medicine cabinet. Cut tiles in both corners should be of similar width to maintain a symmetrical look in the room.

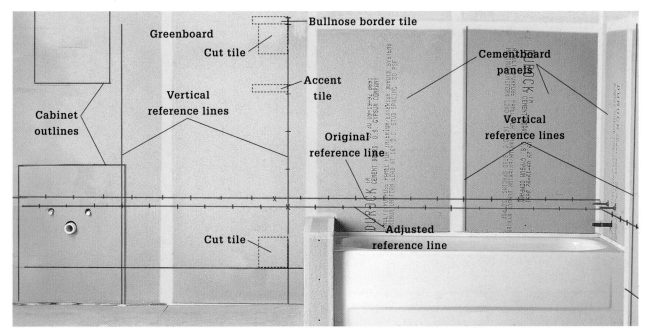

Bullnose border tile

Greenboard

Cut tile

Accent tile

Cementboard panels

Cabinet outlines

Vertical reference lines

Original reference line

Vertical reference lines

Cut tile

Adjusted reference line

The key to a successful wall-tile project is the layout. Mark the wall to show the planned location of all wall cabinets, fixtures, and wall accessories, then locate the most visible horizontal line in the bathroom, which is usually the top edge of the bathtub. Follow the steps on pages 38 to 44 to establish the layout, using a story stick to see how the tile pattern will run in relation to the other features in the room. After establishing the working reference lines, mark additional vertical reference lines on the walls every 5 to 6 tile spaces along the adjusted horizontal reference line to split large walls into smaller, workable quadrants, then install the tile. *Note: Premixed, latex mastic adhesives generally are acceptable for wall tile in dry areas.*

Tiling a Fireplace Surround

Tile dresses a fireplace surround in style—any style you like. From simple ceramic to elegant cut stone to handmade art tile, anything goes. As long as it's sturdy enough to withstand significant swings in temperature, almost any tile will work.

Although the project shown here starts with unfinished wallboard, you can tile over any level surface that's not glossy. If you're tiling over old tile or brick, go over the surface with a grinder, then apply a thin coat of latex-reinforced thinset mortar to even out any irregularities. To rough up painted surfaces, sand them lightly before beginning the project.

The tile shown here is flush with the face of the firebox, which then supports it during installation. If necessary, tack battens in place to support the weight of your tile during installation. (Make sure the batten is level.)

You can finish the edges of the surround with wood cap rail trim, as shown here, bullnose tile, or other trim tile.

Tools & Materials ▸

Level	Tile spacers
Drill	Latex-reinforced
Hammer	thinset mortar
Nail set	Masking tape
Notched trowel	Grout
Grout float	Cap rail trim
2 × 4 lumber	6d and 4d finish nails
Mantel	Wood putty
Tile	Sponge

How to Tile a Fireplace Surround

1

To install the mantel, measure up from the floor and mark the height of the support cleat. Use a level to draw a level line through the mark. Mark the stud locations just above the level line. Position the cleat on the line, centered between the frame sides, and drill a pilot hole at each stud location. Fasten the cleat to the studs with screws provided by the manufacturer.

2

Paint the areas of wallboard that won't be tiled. Finish the mantel as desired, then fit it over the support cleat and center it. Drill pilot holes for 6d finish nails through the top of the mantel, about ¾" from the back edge. Secure the mantel to the cleat with four nails. Set the nails with a nail set, fill the holes with wood putty, then touch up the finish.

3

Dry-fit the tile around the front of the fireplace. You can lay tile over the black front face, but do not cover the glass or any portion of the grills. If you're using tile without spacer lugs, use spacers to set the gaps (at least ⅛" for floor tile). Mark the perimeter of the tile area and make any other layout marks that will help with the installation. Pre-cut tiles, if possible.

4

Mask off around the tile, then use a V-notched trowel to apply latex mastic tile adhesive to the wall, spreading it evenly just inside the perimeter lines. Set the tiles into the adhesive, aligning them with the layout marks, and press firmly to create a good bond. Install spacers as you work, and scrape out excess adhesive from the grout joints. Install all of the tile, then let the adhesive dry completely.

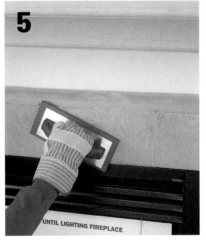

5

Mix a batch of grout and spread it over the tiles with a rubber grout float. Drag the float across the joints diagonally, tilting it at a 45° angle. Make another pass to remove excess grout. Wait 10 to 15 minutes, then wipe away excess grout with a damp sponge, rinsing frequently. Let the grout dry for one hour, then polish the tiles with a dry cloth. Let the grout dry completely.

6

Cut pieces of cap rail trim to fit around the tile, mitering the ends. If the tile is thicker than the trim recesses, install buildup strips behind the trim, using finish nails. Finish the trim to match the mantel. Drill pilot holes and nail the trim in place with 4d finish nails. Set the nails with a nail set. Fill the holes with wood putty and touch up the finish.

Tiling a Kitchen Backsplash

There are few spaces in your home with as much potential for creativity and visual impact as the 18" between your kitchen countertop and cupboards. A well-designed backsplash can transform an ordinary kitchen into something extraordinary. Tiles for the backsplash can be attached directly to wallboard or plaster and do not require backerboard. When purchasing the tile, order 10 percent extra to cover breakage and cutting. Before installing, prepare the work area by removing switch and receptacle coverplates. Protect the countertop from scratches by covering it with a drop cloth.

Tools & Materials ▸

Level	Straight 1 × 2
Tape measure	Wall tile
Pencil	Tile spacers
Tile cutter	(if needed)
Rod saw	Bullnose trim tile
Notched trowel	Mastic tile adhesive
Rubber grout float	Masking tape
Beating block	Grout
Rubber mallet	Caulk
Sponge	Drop cloth
Bucket	Grout sealer

Tips for Planning Tile Layouts ▸

Gather planning brochures and design catalogs to help you create decorative patterns and borders for the backsplash.

Break tiles into fragments and make a mosaic backsplash. Always use a sanded grout for joints wider than ⅛".

Add painted mural tiles to create a focal point. Mixing various tile styles adds an appealing contrast.

How to Tile a Backsplash

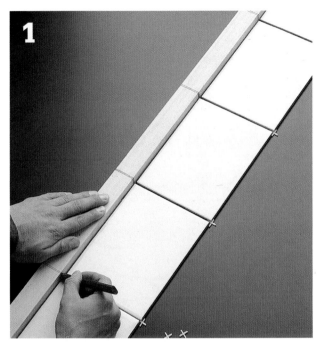

Make a story stick by marking a board at least half as long as the backsplash area to match the tile spacing.

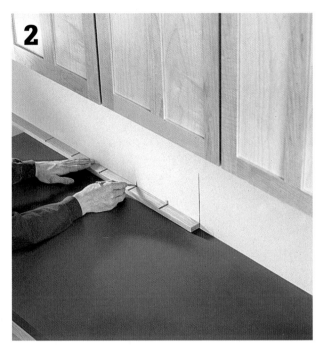

Starting at the midpoint of the installation area, use the story stick to make layout marks along the wall. If an end piece is too small (less than half a tile), adjust the midpoint to give you larger, more attractive end pieces. Use a level to mark this point with a vertical reference line.

While it may appear straight, your countertop may not be level and therefore is not a reliable reference line. Run a level along the counter to find the lowest point on the countertop. Mark a point two tiles up from the low point and extend a level line across the entire work area.

(continued)

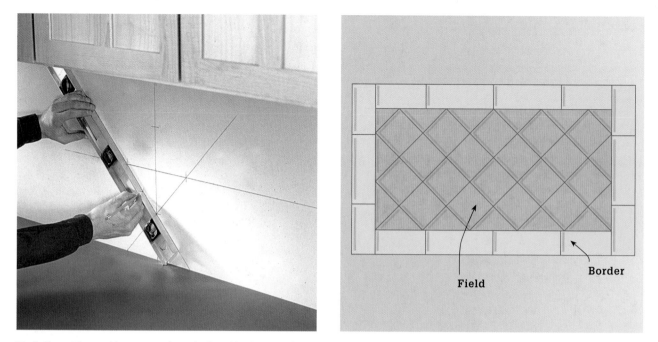

Field

Border

Variation: Diagonal layout. Mark vertical and horizontal reference lines, making sure the angle is 90°. To establish diagonal layout lines, measure out equal distances from the crosspoint, then connect the points with a line. Additional layout lines can be extended from these as needed. To avoid the numerous, unattractive perimeter cuts common to diagonal layouts, try using a standard border pattern as shown. Diagonally set a field of full tiles only, then cut enough half tiles to fill out the perimeter. Finally, border the diagonal field with tiles set square to the field.

4

5

6

Apply mastic adhesive evenly to the area beneath the horizontal reference line, using a notched trowel. Comb the adhesive horizontally with the notched edge.

Starting at the vertical reference line, press tiles into the adhesive with a slight twisting motion. If the tiles are not self-spacing, use plastic spacers to maintain even grout lines. If the tiles do not hang in place, use masking tape to hold them in place until the adhesive sets.

Install a whole row along the reference line, checking occasionally to make sure the tiles are level. Continue installing tiles below the first row, trimming tiles that butt against the countertop as needed.

7

Apply adhesive to an area above the line and continue placing tiles, working from the center to the sides. Install trim tile, such as bullnose tile, to the edges of the rows.

8

When the tiles are in place, make sure they are flat and firmly embedded by laying a beating block against the tile and rapping it lightly with a mallet. Remove the spacers. Allow the mastic to dry for at least 24 hours, or as directed by the manufacturer.

9

Mix the grout and apply it with a rubber grout float. Spread it over the tiles, keeping the float at a low 30° angle, pressing the grout deep into the joints. *Note: For grout joints ⅛" and smaller, be sure to use a non-sanded grout.*

10

Wipe off excess grout, holding the float at a right angle to the tile, working diagonally so as not to remove grout from the joints. Clean any remaining grout from the tiles with a damp sponge, working in a circular motion. Rinse the sponge thoroughly and often.

11

Shape the grout joints by making slow, short, passes with the sponge, shaving down any high spots; rinse the sponge frequently. Fill any voids by applying a dab of grout with your fingertip. When the grout has dried to a haze, buff the tile clean with a soft cloth. Apply a bead of caulk between the countertop and tiles. Reinstall any electrical fixtures you removed. After the grout has completely cured, you may want to apply a grout sealer to help prevent discoloration.

Building a Tiled Wall Niche

A wall niche—a small recessed area between studs—provides ideal display space and creates a focal point in a room. Typical recessed niches require that you cut into the wall, which can be a little intimidating. An easier answer is to build outward from the wall, as we do here.

The "columns" that form the sides of our niche are plain wood boxes that are built in a workshop and then installed. Quartz tile is attached to the columns after installation, and contrasting wall tiles are added to the wallspace between the columns. Finally, glass shelves are installed between the tiled columns to complete the project. The finished look is textural, natural, and sophisticated.

When designing your project, consider the size of the tile and grout lines to create a plan that requires the fewest possible cut tiles. If it's not possible to complete an area (such as a column or the background) with full tile, plan to cut equal-size tiles for each side so the full tiles are centered. If it is not possible for you to attach both boxes to wall studs, use sturdy hollow wall anchors or toggle bolts to secure one of the boxes.

Tools & Materials ▸

Tape measure	Needlenose pliers
Stud finder	Rubber mallet
Circular saw	Four 1 × 6s
Drill	Four 1 × 8s
Long driver bit	1¼" Phillips or square-
or bit extender	head screws
Bar clamps	Construction adhesive
Pry bar	Wide painter's tape
Hammer	Sheet plastic tile
Laser or	Thinset mortar
carpenter's level	Tile spacers
and chalk line	Grout
Awl	Latex additive
¼" carbide-tip bit	Straight 2 × 2 scraps
¼" notched trowel	for battens
Grout float	Shelf pins (4 per shelf)
Grout sponge	Teflon tape
Buff rag	Glass shelves
Foam brush	Grout sealer

How to Build a Tiled Wall Niche

Use a stud finder to locate the studs in the area and mark them. Measure the area and draw a plan on graph paper.

If there are baseboards in the construction area, remove them, using a pry bar and hammer. Tape down sheet plastic in the construction area, as close to the wall as possible.

(continued)

Cut four 1 × 6 and four 1 × 8s to length (108 inches for our project). On two of the 1 × 8s, drill ¾-inch holes centered every 10" down the length of each board. On the remaining two 1 × 8s, drill pilot holes centered every 10".

Place one 1 × 8 (one with pilot holes) on the work surface and position a 1 × 6 on edge beside it. Clamp the boards together and drive a 1¼" screw every 6" to join them. Put a second 1 × 8 (one with ¾" holes) on the work surface and clamp to assembly to it as shown. Drive screws every 6 inches to join the pieces.

Complete the box by adding a 1 × 6 to the opposite side of the assembly and fasten it as described above. Build a second, identical box.

Shoot a vertical line on the wall with the laser level. Spread a bead of construction adhesive on the back (1 × 8 with pilot holes) of the first box. With a helper, align the outside edge of the box. Using a long magnetic driver bit or bit extender, drive an 1¼" screw through each pilot hole (and into stud). Install the second box on the other side of the niche. *Note: When you cannot hit a stud, use toggle bolts.*

Mark the reference lines (see pages 47 through 51). If necessary, tack a 1 × 2 batten in position to support the second row of tile above the floor. If tiles have to be cut for this row, mark and cut all of them (see page 254).

Mix a small batch of thinset mortar. Spread the mortar on a small section of wall, then set the tiles into it. If tile is not self-spacing, insert spacers as you work. When all other tile is set, remove the battens and set the bottom row.

9

Repeat Step 8 to set tile on first one box and then the other. Let the mortar cure, according to manufacturer's instructions.

10

If there are spacers between tiles, use needlenose pliers to remove them. Grout the tile in the center of the niche. If necessary, grout the tile on the columns. (The type of tile shown here does not get grouted.) Let the grout set and then wipe away excess with a damp sponge.

11

On the inside edges of each column, measure and mark the location for the shelf pins. Use a laser level to check and adjust the marks. Using an awl and hammer, create a dimple at each mark, then use a carbide-tipped ¼" bit to drill the holes.

12

Wrap the peg of each shelf pin with Teflon tape. (The tape will seal the hole and keep moisture from getting behind the tile.) Tap a pin into each hole, using a rubber mallet if necessary. Position the glass shelves.

Embellishing a Tiled Wall

Many of us live with tile we don't particularly like. It's easy to see why: builders and remodelers often install simple, neutral tile in an effort not to put anyone off. Older homes sometimes have tile that's not quite vintage but certainly no longer stylish. Or, a previous owner might just have had different tastes. Because tile is so long-lasting, new styles and trends often overtake it and make it look dated. Here's a bit of good news: there's a choice beyond simply living with it or tearing out perfectly good tile to start over.

Removing a section of boring tile and replacing it with some decorative accent tile can transform a plain-Jane wall into one that makes a unique design statement. And while a project like this requires a bit of demolition, it can be done with very little mess and fuss. Because it involves breaking the seal of the wall surface, it's a better choice for a tiled wall that gets little exposure to water (as opposed to a shower wall or tub deck).

The new tile you install will need to be grouted, and the new grout undoubtedly will be a different color. The only way to blend the new tile into the old is to regrout the entire area. If the project involves only one wall and the same grout color is still available, it is necessary to remove the grout surrounding the tile on the project wall. If you are tiling two or more walls, regrout the whole room.

This project is easier if you don't have to cut any existing tile. It's not especially difficult if you do, but it's always best to know what you're getting into before committing to a project.

Tools & Materials ▸

Tape measure	Masking tape
Grout saw	Safety glasses
Grout scraper	Drywall screws
Flat head screwdriver	Cementboard
Straightedge	Construction adhesive
Utility knife	Drywall screws
Drill	Thinset mortar
¼" notched trowel	Mosaic medallion or
Grout float	decorative tile
Grout sponge	Tile spacers
Buff rag	Grout
Foam brush	Latex additive
Needlenose pliers	Grout sealer
Drop cloth	Dust mask
Grease pencil	

How to Embellish a Tiled Wall

Measure the decorative tiles and draw a detailed plan for your project. Indicate a removal area at least one tile larger than the space required. If it will be necessary to cut tile, create a plan that will result in symmetrical tiles.

Protect the floor with a drop cloth. So you can patch the tile backer, you'll need to remove a section of tile that's a minimum of one tile all around the project installation area. Using a grease pencil, mark the tiles to be removed, according to the plan drawing. Put masking tape on the edges of the bordering tiles that will remain to keep them from being scratched or otherwise damaged by the grout saw. If you will be reinstalling some of the old tiles, protect them as well.

(continued)

3

Wearing eye protection and a dust mask, use a grout saw to cut grooves in all of the grout lines in the removal area. If the grout lines are soft this will only take one or two passes. If the grout's hard, it may take several. Using a grout scraper, remove any remaining material in the joint. Angle the tools toward the open area to protect the tile.

4

With a flathead screwdriver, pry up the edges of the tile at the center of the removal area. Wiggle the blade toward the center of the tile and pry up to pop it off. (For large areas, see page 243 for another removal method.)

5

Draw cutting lines on the drywall that are at least ½" inside the borders of the area where you removed tiles. Using a straightedge and utility knife, carefully cut out the old drywall. If the tile comes off very easily and the tile backer is not damaged, you may be able to scrape it clean and reuse it.

6

Cut cementboard strips that are slightly longer than the width of the opening. Insert the strips into the opening and orient them so the ends are pressed against the back surface of the tile backer. Drive wallboard screws through the edges of the old tile backer and into the strips to hold them in place.

7

Cut a cementboard patch to fit the opening in the tile backer. Place the patch in the opening and drive drywall screws through the cementboard and into the backer strips. Also drive screws at any stud locations.

8

Cover the edges with wallboard tape. Mix a small batch of thinset mortar (see page 260). Apply the mortar, using a notched trowel to spread it evenly.

Gently press the accent tiles into the adhesive, smoothing it from the center toward the edges. Let the mortar cure as directed.

Use a damp sponge to soak the protective sheet on the tile. Once wet, slide the sheet off and throw it away.

Mix a batch of grout and fill the joints between tile on the entire wall, one section at a time (see page 60). (Inset) Clean the tile with a damp sponge. Occasionally rinse the sponge in cool water.

Design Suggestions ▸

Inserts add interest, texture, and color to tile designs. This piece combines tumbled stone with marble in a delicate floral motif.

This stone insert adds a contemporary flair to a simple tile design.

Building a Tiled Tub Deck

The aprons that are cast into alcove bathtubs simplify the tub installation, but they often come up a bit short in the style department. One way to improve the appearance of a plain apron and create the look of a built-in tub is simply to build and tile a short wall in front of the tub. All it takes is a little simple framing and a few square feet of tile.

The basic strategy is to construct a 2 × 4 stub wall in front of the tub apron and then tile the top and front of the wall. One design option is to try and match existing tile, but it's unlikely you'll be able to find the exact tile unless it's relatively new. Choosing complementary or contrasting tile is usually a better bet. Specialty tile, such as listellos, pencils, and accent tile, can create a lot of impact without breaking the bank because you're covering such a small area. Ask your tile retailer to direct you to families of tile with multiple shapes and accessories.

Be sure to include a waterproof backer (cementboard is recommended) and get a good grout seal, since the stub wall will be in a wet area.

Tools & Materials ▸

Stud finder	2½" screws
Tape measure	Cementboard
Circular saw	Drywall screws
Drill	Tile
Hammer	Thinset mortar
Laser or	Scrap of carpet
carpenter's level	Carbide paper
Tile cutting tools	or wet stone
Utility knife	Wide painter's tape
Grout float	Grout
Grout sponge	Silicone caulk
Buff rag	Grout sealer
Foam brush	Permanent marker
2 × 4 lumber	Notched trowel
Construction adhesive	Rubbing alcohol

How to Build a Tiled Tub Deck

1

Measure the distance of the tub rim from the floor, as well as the distance from one wall to the other at the ends of the tub. Allowing for the thickness of the tiles, create a layout for the project and draw a detailed plan for your project, spacing the studs 16" apart on center.

2

Cut the 2 × 4s to length for the base plate and top plate (58½" long as shown). Cut the studs (five 11" pieces as shown). Set the base plate on edge and lay out the studs, spacing them 16" on center. Make sure the first and last studs are perfectly parallel with the end of the base plate, then drive two 2½" screws through the base plate and each stud.

3

Draw a placement line on the floor, using a permanent marker. Spread a generous bead of construction adhesive on the bottom of the base plate. Align the base plate with the placement line and set it into position. Put concrete blocks or other weights between the studs to anchor the base plate to the flooring and let the adhesive cure according to manufacturer's instructions.

4

Drive two or three 2½" screws through the studs and into the room walls at each end of the stub wall. If the stub wall does not happen to line up with any wall studs, at least drive two 3" deck screws toenail style through the stub wall and into the room wall sole plate.

(continued)

Set the top plate on the stud wall and attach it, using two 2½" screws for each stud. Offset the screws slightly to increase the strength of the assembly. The top of the stud wall should be 2½" below the top of the tub.

Cut cementboard to fit the front (14½" as shown). With the factory-finished edge of the cementboard at the top of the wall, attach the cementboard to the studs, using drywall screws (see page 246).

Cut cementboard to fit the top of the stub wall (3½"). With the factory-finished edge facing the tub edge, attach the cement board to the top plate, using drywall screws.

Design the layout and mark reference lines (see page 41) on the wall. Draw horizontal and vertical reference lines for the corner tile (used to transition from vertical to horizontal at the top stub wall edge) and the coved base tile (if your project includes them, as ours does). Lay out tile along the floor, including spacers.

9

Start tiling at the bottom of the wall. Lay out the bottom row of tile on the floor, using spacers if necessary. Adjust the layout to make end tiles balanced in size. Mark and cut the tiles as necessary, and then smooth any sharp edges with carbide paper or a wet stone. Mix a small batch of thinset mortar (see page 260) and install the base tiles by buttering the backs with mortar (see page 261).

10

Beginning at the center intersection of the vertical field area, apply mortar, using a notched trowel to spread it evenly. Cover as much area as required for a few field tiles. Install the field tiles, keeping the grout lines in alignment.

11

Finish installing the field tiles up to the horizontal line marking the accent tile location.

12

Apply thinset mortar to the backs of the accent tiles and install them in a straight line. The grout lines will likely not align with the field tile grout lines.

(continued)

Install corner tiles to create a rounded transition at the top edge of the wall. Install these before you install the filed tiles in the top row of the wall face or on the top of the stub wall (corner tiles are virtually impossible to cut if your measurements are off). Dry-lay the top row of tiles. Mark and cut tile if necessary.

Fill in the top course of field tile on the wall face, between the accent tiles and the corner tiles. If you have planned well you won't need to trim the field tiles to fit. (If you need to cut tiles to create the correct wall height, choose the tiles in the first row of field tiles.)

Remove the dry-lay row of tile along the top of the wall. Shield the edge of the tub with painter's tape, then spread thinset adhesive on the wall and begin to lay tile. Keep the joints of the field tiles on the top aligned with the grout joints of the field tile on the face of the wall.

Mix a batch of grout and use a grout float to force it into the joints between the tiles. Keep the space between the top field tiles and the tub clear of grout to create space for a bead of silicone caulk between the tub and tile.

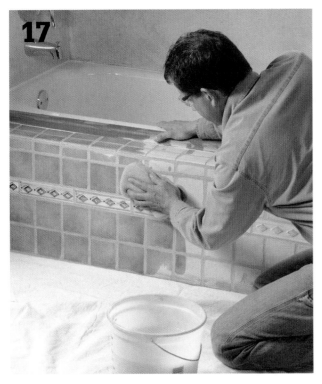

Remove excess grout and clean the tile using a damp sponge. Rinse the sponge often.

After 24 hours, clean the area where the tile and tub meet with rubbing alcohol, then put tape on the edge of the tub and the face of the tile. Apply clear silicone caulk into the gap, overfilling it slightly.

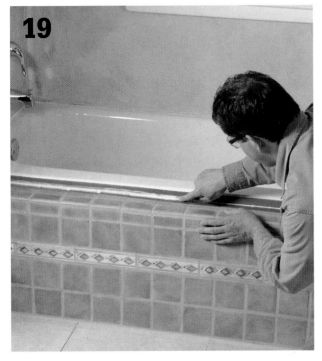

Smooth the caulk with a moistened plastic straw or a moistened fingertip to create an even finish. Make sure this spot is well-sealed, as it is a prime spot for water to penetrate into the tub wall.

When the grout has cured completely (consult manufacturer's directions), apply grout sealer to the joints.

Countertop Projects

Tile countertops are a cook's dream—resistant to heat and stains, easy to clean, and extremely durable. Fortunately, the process of building one is much easier than most people would imagine. The projects included in this chapter lead you through constructing the countertop itself as well as tiling it, and all the way through setting tile on a bi-level countertop and backsplash.

Edge treatments are integral parts of a countertop design. Consider trim tile, wood, and other material options for your edges and be sure to create a layout that complements the treatment you choose.

When designing a countertop, remember that larger tiles produce fewer grout lines to keep clean and more stable surfaces. For work areas, flat tiles are better than tiles with rounded or beveled edges because bowls and pans rock on rounded edges.

Before selecting natural stone tile for countertops, research your choice carefully. Some natural stone stains and scratches easily and requires more maintenance than you might wish to invest in a countertop. Be especially careful about choosing porous stone, which is difficult to keep clean in a kitchen or bathroom environment.

In This Chapter:

- Building a Tile Countertop
- Building a Tiled Bi-Level Island

Geometric accent tiles draw all eyes to this backsplash and countertop made of natural looking porcelain tile.

Solid blue V-cap anchors the edges of this blue and white countertop to the wall below. The same blue is repeated on the tub surround and the mirror frame.

The decorative border at this counter's edge is repeated from the border at the base of the backsplash. This strategy tricks the eye into seeing the decorative edge as part of the border from some angles.

V-cap protects the edges of this countertop and blends its color into the wood trim and the sleek cabinets below.

Here, white on white is the theme, presenting a clean, crisp background that can be accessorized in many ways over time. The textures in the wall tile and the profile of this countertop's V-cap keep this minimalist approach from becoming boring.

The countertops on this kitchen island complement the wallpaper borders on the soffit and inside the recessed ceiling.

The mosaic tile on this countertop produces an interesting coherence for the overall room design.

Attractive edge treatments complete tile countertops. Here, a wood treatment is stained to complement the woodwork of the cabinets and the adjoining room.

Building a Tile Countertop

Ceramic and porcelain tile remain popular choices for countertops and backsplashes for a number of reasons: It's available in a vast range of sizes, styles, and colors; it's durable and repairable; and some tile—not all—is reasonably priced. With careful planning, tile is also easy to install, making a custom countertop a good do-it-yourself project.

The best tile for most countertops is glazed ceramic or porcelain floor tile. Glazed tile is better than unglazed because of its stain resistance, and floor tile is better than wall tile because it's thicker and more durable.

While glazing protects tile from stains, the grout between tiles is still vulnerable because it's so porous. To minimize staining, use a grout that contains a latex additive, or mix the grout using a liquid latex additive. After the grout cures fully, apply a quality grout sealer, and reapply the sealer once a year thereafter. Choosing larger tiles reduces the number of grout lines. Although the selection is a bit limited, if you choose 13" × 13" floor tile, you can span from the front to the back edge of the countertop with a single seam.

The countertop in this project has a substrate of ¾" exterior-grade plywood that's cut to fit and fastened to the cabinets. The plywood is covered with a layer of plastic (for a moisture barrier) and a layer of ½"-thick cementboard. Cementboard is an effective backer for tile because it won't break down if water gets through the tile layer. The tile is adhered to the cementboard with thinset adhesive. The overall thickness of the finished countertop is about 1½". If you want a thicker countertop, you can fasten an additional layer of plywood (of any thickness) beneath the substrate. Two layers of ¾" exterior-grade plywood without cementboard is also an acceptable substrate.

You can purchase tiles made specifically to serve as backsplashes and front edging. While the color and texture may match, these tiles usually come in only one length, making it difficult to get your grout lines to align with the field tiles. You can solve this problem by cutting your own edging and backsplash tiles from field tiles (see step 5, page 108).

Tools & Materials ▶

Tape measure	Tile spacers
Circular saw	¾" exterior-grade
Drill	(CDX) plywood
Utility knife	4-mil polyethylene
Straightedge	sheeting
Stapler	Packing tape
Drywall knife	½" cementboard
Framing square	1¼" galvanized deck screws
Notched trowel	Fiberglass mesh tape
Tile cutter	Thinset mortar
Carpeted 2 × 4	Grout with latex additive
Mallet	Silicone caulk
Rubber grout float	Silicone grout sealer
Sponge	Tile saw
Foam brush	Grout float
Caulk gun	Metal ruler
Ceramic tile	Writing utensil

Ceramic or porcelain makes a durable countertop that is heat-resistant and relatively easy for a DIYer to create. By using larger tiles, you minimize the grout lines (and the cleaning that goes with them).

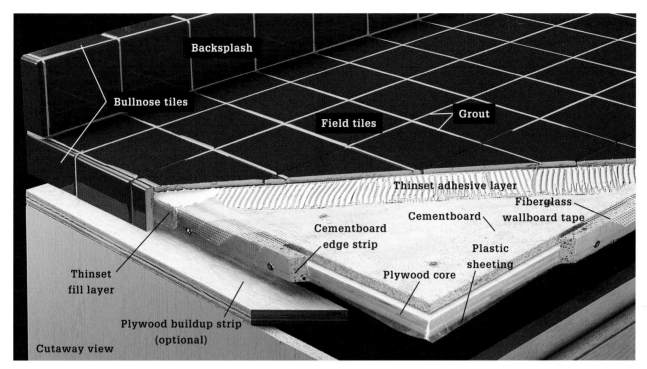

A ceramic tile countertop made with wall tile starts with a core of ¾" exterior-grade plywood that's covered with a moisture barrier of 4-mil polyethylene sheeting. Half-inch cementboard is screwed to the plywood, and the edges are capped with cementboard and finished with fiberglass mesh tape and thinset mortar. Tiles for edging and backsplashes may be bullnose or trimmed from the factory edges of field tiles.

Options for Backsplashes & Countertop Edges

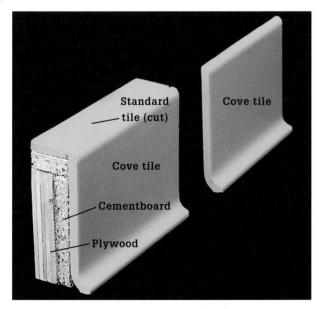

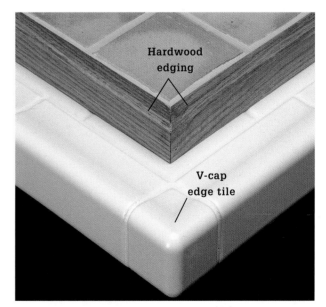

Backsplashes can be made from cove tile attached to the wall at the back of the countertop. You can use the tile alone or build a shelf-type backsplash, using the same construction as for the countertop. Attach the plywood backsplash to the plywood core of the countertop. Wrap the front face and all edges of the plywood backsplash with cementboard before laying tile.

Edge options include V-cap edge tile and hardwood strip edging. V-cap tiles have raised and rounded corners that create a ridge around the countertop perimeter—good for containing spills and water. V-cap tiles must be cut with a tile saw. Hardwood strips should be prefinished with at least three coats of polyurethane finish. Attach the strips to the plywood core so the top of the wood will be flush with the faces of the tiles.

Tips for Laying Out Tile ▶

- You can lay tile over a laminate countertop that's square, level, and structurally sound. Use a belt sander with 60- or 80-grit sandpaper to rough up the surface before setting the tiles. The laminate cannot have a no-drip edge. If you're using a new substrate and need to remove your existing countertop, make sure the base cabinets are level front to back, side to side, and with adjoining cabinets. Unscrew a cabinet from the wall and use shims on the floor or against the wall to level it, if necessary.

- Installing battens along the front edge of the countertop helps ensure the first row of tile is perfectly straight. For V-cap tiles, fasten a 1 × 2 batten along the reference line, using screws. The first row of field tile is placed against this batten. For bullnose tiles, fasten a batten that's the same thickness as the edging tile, plus ⅛" for mortar thickness, to the face of the countertop so the top is flush with the top of the counter. The bullnose tiles are aligned with the outside edge of the batten. For wood edge trim, fasten a 1 × 2 batten to the face of the countertop so the top edge is above the top of the counter. The tiles are installed against the batten.

- Before installing any tile, lay out the tiles in a dry run using spacers. If your counter is L-shaped, start at the corner and work outward. Otherwise, start the layout at a sink to ensure equal-sized cuts on both sides of the sink. If necessary, shift your starting point so you don't end up cutting very narrow tile segments.

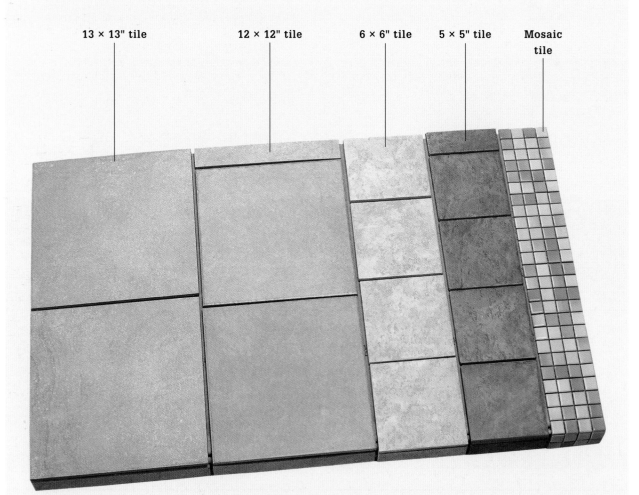

13 × 13" tile   **12 × 12" tile**   **6 × 6" tile**   **5 × 5" tile**   **Mosaic tile**

The bigger the tile the fewer the grout lines. If you want a standard 25"-deep countertop, the only way to get there without cutting tiles is to use mosaic strips or 1" tile. With 13 × 13" tile, you need to trim 1" off the back tile but have only one grout line front to back. As you decrease tile size, the number of grout lines increases.

How to Build a Tile Countertop

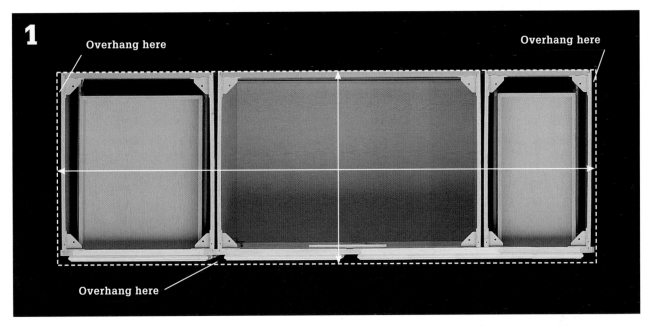

1

Overhang here

Overhang here

Overhang here

Determine the size of the plywood substrate by measuring across the top of the cabinets. The finished top should overhang the drawer fronts by at least ¼". Be sure to account for the thickness of the cementboard, adhesive, and tile when deciding how large to make the overhang. Cut the substrate to size from ¾" plywood, using a circular saw. Also make any cutouts for sinks and other fixtures.

2

Corner bracket

Set the plywood substrate on top of the cabinets, and attach it with screws driven through the cabinet corner brackets. The screws should not be long enough to go through the top of the substrate.

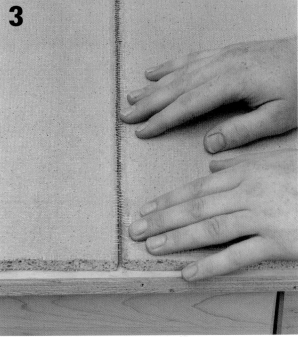

3

Cut pieces of cementboard to size, then mark and make the cutout for the sink. Dry-fit them on the plywood core with the rough sides of the panels facing up. Leave a ⅛" gap between the cementboard sheets and a ¼" gap along the perimeter.

(continued)

Option: Cut cementboard using a straightedge and utility knife or a cementboard cutter with a carbide tip. Hold the straightedge along the cutting line, and score the board several times with the knife. Bend the piece backward to break it along the scored line. Back-cut to finish.

Lay the 4-mil plastic moisture barrier over the plywood substrate, draping it over the edges. Tack it in place with a few staples. Overlap seams in the plastic by 6", and seal them with packing tape.

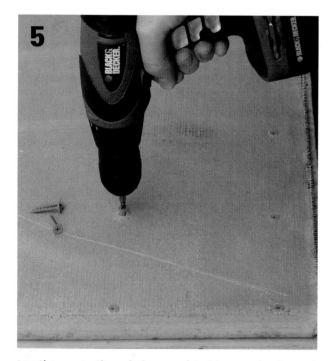

Lay the cementboard pieces rough-side up on the plywood and attach them with cementboard screws driven every 6". Drill pilot holes using a masonry bit, and make sure all screw heads are flush with the surface. Wrap the countertop edges with 1¼"-wide cementboard strips, and attach them to the core with cementboard screws.

Tape all cementboard joints with fiberglass mesh tape. Apply three layers of tape along the front edge where the horizontal cementboard sheets meet the cementboard edging.

7

Fill all gaps and cover all of the tape with a layer of thinset mortar. Feather out the mortar with a drywall knife to create a smooth, flat surface.

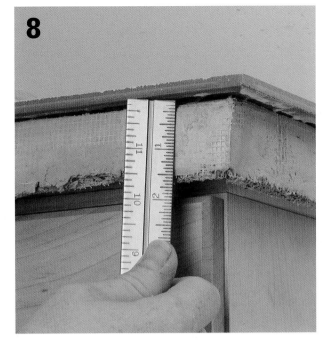

8

Determine the required width of your edge tiles. Lay a field tile onto the tile base so it overhangs the front edge by ½" or so. Then, hold a metal ruler up to the underside of the tile and measure the distance from the tile to the bottom of the subbase. Your edge tiles should be cut to this width. (The gap for the grout line will cause the edge tile to extend past the subbase, concealing it completely.)

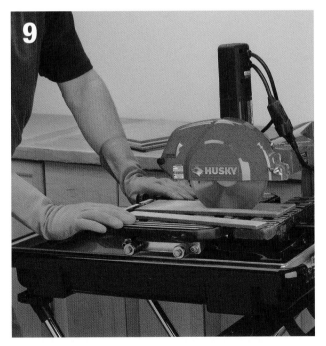

9

Cut your edge tiles to the determined width, using a tile saw. It's worth renting a quality wet saw for tile if you don't own one. Floor tile is thick and difficult to cut with a hand cutter (especially porcelain tiles).

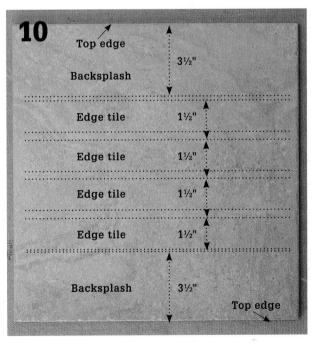

10

Top edge

Backsplash — 3½"

Edge tile — 1½"

Edge tile — 1½"

Edge tile — 1½"

Edge tile — 1½"

Backsplash — 3½"

Top edge

Cut tiles for the backsplash. The backsplash tiles (3½" wide in our project) should be cut with a factory edge on each tile that will be oriented upward when they're installed. You can make efficient use of your tiles by cutting edge tiles from the center area of the tiles you cut to make the backsplash.

(continued)

Sink cutout area

Dry-fit tiles on the countertop to find the layout that works best. Once the layout is established, make marks along the vertical and horizontal rows. Draw reference lines through the marks and use a framing square to make sure the lines are perpendicular.

Variation: Laying Out with Small Floor Tiles and Bullnose Edging ▶

Lay out tiles and spacers in a dry run. Adjust starting lines, if necessary. If using battens, lay the field tile flush with the battens, then apply edge tile. Otherwise, install the edging first. If the countertop has an inside corner, start there by installing a ready-made inside corner or cutting a 45° miter in edge tile to make your own inside corner.

Place the first row of field tile against the edge tile, separating the tile with spacers. Lay out the remaining rows of tile. Adjust starting lines if necessary to create a layout using the least number of cut tiles.

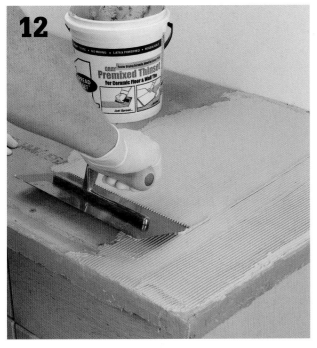

12

Use a ⅜" square notched trowel to apply a layer of thinset adhesive to the cementboard. Apply enough for two or three tiles, starting at one end. Hold the trowel at roughly a 30-degree angle and try not to overwork the adhesive or remove too much.

13

Set the first tile into the adhesive. Hold a piece of the edge tile against the countertop edge as a guide to show you exactly how much the tile should overhang the edge.

14

Cut all the back tiles for the layout to fit (you'll need to remove about 1" of a 13 × 13" tile) before you begin the actual installation. Set the back tiles into the thinset, maintaining the gap for groutlines created by the small spacer nubs cast into the tiles. If your tiles have no spacer nubs, see next step.

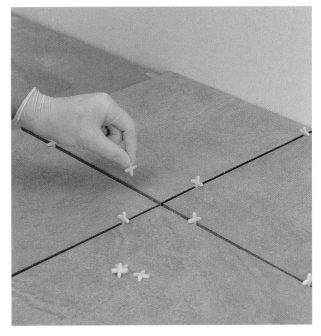

Option: To maintain even grout lines, some beginning tilers insert plus-sign shaped plastic spacers at the joints. This is less likely to be useful with large tiles like those shown here, but it is effective. Many tiles today feature built-in spacing lugs, so the spacers are of no use. Make sure to remove the spacers before the thinset sets. If you leave them in place they will corrupt your grout lines.

(continued)

Variation: To mark border tiles for cutting, allow space for backsplash tiles, grout, and mortar by placing a tile against the back wall. Set another tile (A) on top of the last full tile in the field, then place a third tile (B) over tile A and hold it against the upright tile. Mark and cut tile A and install it with the cut edge toward the wall. Finish filling in your field tiles.

To create a support ledge for the edge tiles, prop pieces of 2 × 4 underneath the front edge of the substrate overhang, using wood scraps to prop the ledge tightly up against the substrate.

Apply a thick layer of thinset to the backside of the edge tile with your trowel. This is called "buttering" and it is easier and neater than attempting to trowel adhesive onto the countertop edge. Press the tiles into position so they are flush with the leading edges of the field tiles.

Butter each backsplash tile and press it into place, doing your best to keep all of the grout lines aligned.

Mix a batch of grout to complement the tile (keeping in mind that darker grout won't look dirty as soon as lighter grout). Apply the grout to the grout line areas with a grout float.

Let the grout dry until a light film is created on the countertop surface and then wipe the excess grout off with a sponge and warm, clean water.

After the grout has dried (and before you use the sink, if possible) run a bead of clear silicone caulk along the joint between the backsplash and the wall. Install your sink and faucet.

Wait at least one week and then seal the grout lines with a penetrating grout sealer. This is important to do. Sealing the tiles themselves is not a good idea unless you are using unglazed tiles (a poor choice for countertops, however).

Building a Tiled Bi-Level Island

Islands are one of the most requested kitchen features. People love them for many reasons, including their value as bi-level counter space. In most cases, the lower level is used as work space and the upper as casual dining space. The upper level provides a little camouflage for the work space, something that's especially welcome in open-plan kitchens where meal preparation areas can be seen from other areas.

When planning casual dining space, remember that designers suggest at least 24" per person. For the work space, remember that standard design guidelines recommend at least 36" of uninterrupted work space to the side of a sink or cooktop.

On work surfaces, mosaic and other small tile is rarely the best choice. Larger tile requires fewer grout lines, always a good idea when it comes to cleaning and maintenance. But there is no rule that all three elements of a bi-level island have to use the same material. In fact, projects like this offer wonderful opportunities to mix materials or colors or textures. Choose floor tile or tile made especially for counters for the horizontal surfaces, and then branch out when it comes to the backsplash. Wall tile and mosaics work beautifully.

Tools & Materials ▸

Tape measure	Tile spacers
Circular saw	¾" exterior-grade
Drill	(CDX) plywood
Utility knife	4-mil polyethylene
Straightedge	sheeting
Stapler	Packing tape
Drywall knife	½" cementboard
Framing square	1¼" deck screws
Notched trowel	3" deck screws
Tile cutter	Fiberglass mesh tape
Carpeted 2 × 4	Thinset mortar
Mallet	Grout with latex
Rubber grout float	additive
Sponge	Silicone caulk
Foam brush	Silicone grout sealer
Caulk gun	L-brackets
Birch plywood	6d finish nails
1 × 2 hardwood	Drywall screws
2 × 4 lumber	Glue
Ceramic tile	

How to Build a Tiled Bi-Level Island

Build a 2 × 4 base for the island cabinet by cutting the 2 × 4s to length and joining them in a square frame that lays flat (wide sides down) on the floor. Use metal L-brackets to reinforce the joints. If you don't wish to move the island, fasten the frame to the floor in position with construction adhesive and/or deck screws.

Cut bottom panels the same dimensions as the base frame from ¾" birch plywood. Attach it to the frame with finish nails. Then, cut the side panels to size and shape and fasten them to the edges of the curb with 6d finish nails and adhesive. Slip ¾" shims (scrap plywood works well) beneath the side panels before fastening them.

Cut the 2 × 4 cross supports to length and install them between the side panels at every corner, including the corners created by the L-shape cutout. Use 3" deck screws driven through the side panels and into the ends of the cross supports.

Prime and paint the cabinet interior and exterior.

(continued)

Build a face frame from 1 × 2 hardwood to fit the cabinet front. Attach it to the cabinet with 6d finish nails and hang cabinet doors (we installed three 13"-wide overlay doors).

Cut strips of ¾" exterior plywood to make the subbases for the countertops and a backer for the backsplash. The lower counter subbase should over hang by 2" on the front and sides. The upper should overhang 2" on the sides and be centered on the cabinet front to back. Attach the backer and subbases with drywall screws driven down into the 2 × 4 cross supports.

Cut 2" wide strips of plywood for buildup strips and attach to the undersides of the subbases with glue and screws.

Attach tile backerboard to the counter subbases and the backsplash and tape seams and cover screws heads with compound (see page 244).

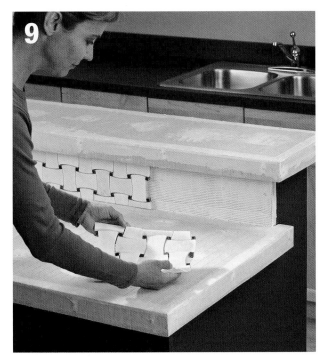

Cut mosaic sheets to fit the backsplash area and attach them with thinset adhesive (see Tiling a Backsplash, page 106).

Cut edge tiles and fasten them around the perimeter of the subbase with thinset adhesive. The tiles should be flush or slightly below the bottoms of the buildup strips, and project past the top surfaces so they will be level with the field tiles. If you are not using edge tiles with a bullnose top, install the tiles so they are level with the subbase surface and overhang them with the field tiles.

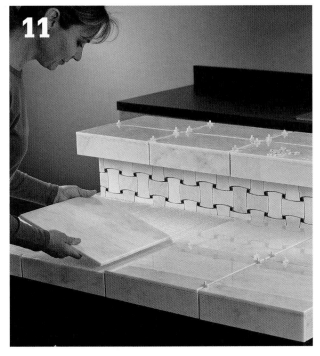

Install the field tiles for the countertops last (see Building Tile Countertops, pages 130 to 139).

Choose a suitable grout color and apply it to the tile with a grout float. Buff off excess once it has dried. Seal the grout with grout sealer.

Decorative Projects

Decorative projects are just plain fun. Once you understand the basic techniques, the possibilities are limited only by your imagination (and quite probably your budget).

In this chapter you'll find projects ranging from small items, such as decorative planters and an address marker to large ones, such as a tiled sink base. You'll see how to frame a bathroom mirror with tile and how to create an artistic mosaic wall-hanging. In short, there's something here for almost everyone.

You'll also find detailed instructions on how to make your own tile. This is an easy process, and one that can be shared with children of all ages. It does require access to a kiln and glazes, but, with some advance notice, that can be arranged with retail pottery shops or studios. This is the type of project that calls out for experimentation and test runs. Try out different shapes and colors; work with traditional and non-traditional tools to create texture; blend glazes until you find a combination that pleases you.

As your skills and confidence grow, you'll discover that decorative tile projects make excellent gifts.

In This Chapter:

- Creating Decorative Planters
- Framing a Bathroom Mirror
- Creating an Address Marker Mosaic
- Creating a Mosaic Wall-hanging
- Building a Tiled Sink Base
- Making Handmade Tile

Tile makes perfect coasters—no finish-damaging moisture can get past these charming little glass tile mosaics.

Lush floral photo murals sparkle against white tile backgrounds in this exotic bathroom.

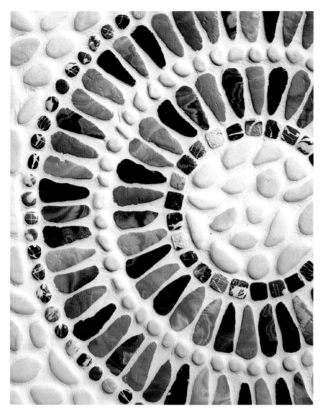

Small mosaic art tiles lie among concentric circles of stone and shards. This idea could be translated to stepping stones, patios, or tabletops—let your imagination be your guide.

The arm of this concrete garden bench holds a broken tile mosaic that combines the colors of water and sun.

Framing a mirror like this one is an artful weekend project. Tile can be placed directly on the mirror (as shown in the project on page 155) or to the wall around the mirror.

A broken tile mosaic transforms this small table into a unique accent piece. Tile can be applied to an existing tabletop or to a top cut from plywood.

This plaster pedestal is decorated with whole and broken tiles. The scrollwork areas are painted with sanded grout that has been thinned with water.

A single hand-decorated tile adorns this iron table frame.

This doorway trim is more ambitious than most decorative projects, but it's quite simple. Just set one row of tile around the doorway and finish the edges with wood trim. Outstanding!

For all practical purposes, typical stair risers are invisible. With their colorful handpainted tile, these risers are anything but typical and certainly not invisible.

Mosaic tile can be pulled from its mesh backing and used to decorate pots and planters, with or without additional broken bits of tile.

This terra-cotta saucer covered with mosaic tile showcases a few blossoms from the garden. It makes an equally interesting birdbath or holder for floating candles.

This lovely piece of artwork began as an inexpensive glass vase. It's easiest to glue tile fragments to pieces like this with hot glue or silicone caulk rather than traditional tile adhesives.

Creating Decorative Planters

The basic steps for adding tile to a planter are much the same as for adding tile to any other surface: Plan the layout, set and grout the tile. Fun and creativity come into the process when you turn your imagination loose with tile and containers.

Don't limit yourself to tile—mix in other materials such as flat glass marbles or broken pieces of stained glass, mirror, and china. The designs can be as simple or as elaborate as you'd like.

Try a mosaic of daisies using bits of white stained glass for the petals, golden flat glass marbles for the centers, and broken tile bits for the background. Or maybe you'd prefer to use bits of green tile for a vine and leaves with purple flat glass marbles arranged like a bunch of grapes. Add a background of broken china or broken stained glass, and you've got a lot to show for a few hours' work.

Select containers that have flat rims like the white planter shown below or that have a broad expanse of flat surface like the pot shown in the project on page 153. Try to match the style and colors of the planters to the design.

Tools & Materials ▸

Snap cutter
Tile nippers
Putty knife
Grout float
Grout sponge

1" mosaic tile
Tile mastic
Grout
Grout sealer

How to Decorate Planters

Remove the mosaic tiles from their backing and experiment with designs and layouts. Cut tiles in half as necessary, using a snap cutter. Use tile nippers to break some tiles into small pieces.

Draw an irregular border around the planter, ranging from 1½" to 2" wide. Use a putty knife to spread mastic within the border and position the tile, alternating between the whole and half tiles all the way around the planter.

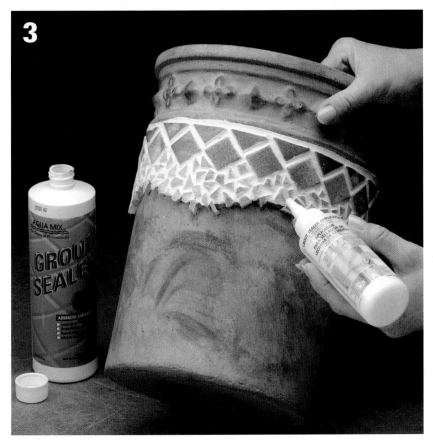

Fill in the remaining portion of the border with pieces of broken tile. Let the mastic dry according to manufacturer's directions. Grout the tile (see page 60 for information on grouting tile). If the planter will be used outdoors, apply grout sealer after the grout has fully cured.

Framing a Bathroom Mirror

The vast majority of bathrooms in new homes these days come equipped with flat, boring mirrors. There's nothing wrong with these mirrors, but there's not much right with them, either. Framing a mirror with ceramic tile transforms it from flat to fabulous, and the whole project takes only a few hours.

The process is extremely simple. In fact, shopping for the tile can be the most difficult part of the project. If you're tiling the rest of the bathroom at the same time, you'll want to combine trim pieces that match or complement the field tile. If the room has no other tile, you can mix and match to your heart's content, going as crazy or as subtle as you like.

There are two ways you can go about tiling a mirror frame: apply the tile directly to the mirror; or tile around the mirror and butt up to the edges. We chose to remove the mirror, attach the tiles around the perimeter, and then rehang the mirror. If you're rehanging a mirror, take care to make sure the hanger and anchor you use are quite sturdy, as the mirror will have put on a good deal of weight.

Tools & Materials ▶

Tape measure
Permanent marker
Wet saw
Laser or
   carpenter's level
Putty knife
Grout float
Grout sponge

Foam paintbrush
Heavy brown paper
   or cardboard
Trim tile
Windshield adhesive
Wide painter's tape
Grout with latex additive
Grout sealer

How to Frame a Bathroom Mirror

Measure the mirror and cut a template from a piece of heavy brown paper or cardboard. Put the template on the floor or a large work surface. Dry lay the tile around it, using spacers if the tiles are not self-spaced.

Mark any tiles that must be cut to produce full tiles at the corners. (If it's absolutely necessary to trim corner tiles, make them all equal lengths.) Miter the one end of each corner tile at a 45° angle (see pages 254 through 259).

(continued)

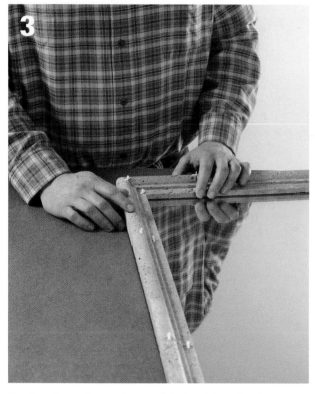

Dry lay the outermost row of chair rail tiles. Check corner miters of chair rail to make sure everything is cut properly and aligned on the mirror as desired.

Starting in the left-hand corner, dry lay the next couple of rows of field tile. For accurate placement, include spacers. Make sure tiles match in corners.

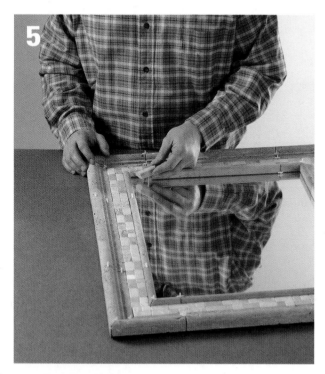

Now that the chair rail and two rows of field tile are aligned, dry lay the final row of pencil tiles. Cut tiles, as necessary, to fit onto mirror as planned. Once all tiles fit as planned, remove all but the first row of chair rail tile.

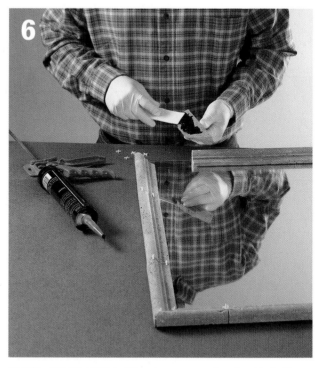

Starting at the top, left-hand corner, apply adhesive to the back of the tile using a small putty knife. Set the tile on the mirror and twist it a little to secure it in place.

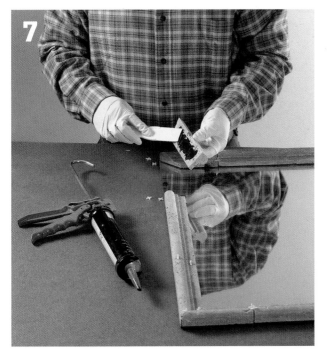

Continue to set the tiles in each corner and then work around the entire perimeter, fastening each tile with adhesive. Once the chair rail is secure, move on to the next row. Repeat this process until all rows are secured to the mirror.

Prepare a small bath of grout and fill all the tile joints. Clean and buff the tile.

Tiled Mirror Designs ▸

In this project, tile is added only to the mirror. The mirror is framed by a mosaic of shards and small pieces of glass tile. Mosaic projects are incredibly easy to do and really add a lot to a small room like this one.

In new construction or major remodeling projects, place the mirror so the trim tile can be attached to the wall rather than to the mirror.

Creating an Address Marker Mosaic

Broken tile and broken china combine beautifully for mosaics of all sorts. Here they're put to work on an address marker, a quick and easy project and a good way to use leftover tile.

Cut the marker in the shape shown here or create your own. No matter what shape you make it, be sure to use exterior-grade plywood and to seal the grout after it has cured according to manufacturer's directions. With those precautions, your address marker will remain attractive for many years.

Tools & Materials ▸

Jigsaw	¾" exterior-grade plywood
Paintbrush	Wood sealer
Rubber mallet	4" number stencils
Tile nippers	Tile
Rotary tool	Chintz-patterned plates
Hot glue gun	Hot glue or silicone caulk
Grout float	Grout
Drill	Slot hangers and screws
Grinding disc	

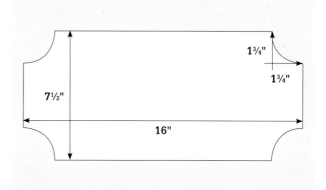

How to Make an Address Marker

Enlarge and photocopy the pattern on the opposite page. Trace the pattern onto plywood and cut it out, using a jigsaw. Apply a coat of wood sealer and let it dry. Mark the center and draw parallel placement lines on the plywood, then plan the placement of the numbers. Trace the numbers onto the plywood, then draw a 1¼" border around the outside edge.

Use a rotary tool and a grinding disc to polish away the ridge on the back of each plate. One at a time, place the plates in a heavy paper bag and roll the top closed. Rap the bag with a rubber mallet to break the plate. (Wear safety goggles.) Break the tiles in the same manner.

Lay out the pieces within the number outlines, using tile nippers to reshape pieces as necessary. Use hot glue or silicone caulk to secure the tile to the plywood. Fill in the background with pieces of china.

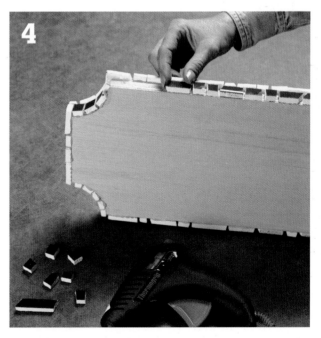

Turn the marker on edge and add tile to all the edges. Grout the tile, let it dry thoroughly, and seal the grout with grout sealer. (See page 60 for more information on grouting tile.) Attach two slot hangers to the back of the mosaic.

Creating a Mosaic Wall-hanging

Unlike most tile projects, a wall-hanging doesn't need to be watertight or have structural strength, so making one gives you the chance to play with tile and other complementary materials. You can use tile fragments, broken dishes, pieces of mirror, and even pieces of glass.

These days it can be difficult to find small pieces of Masonite in building centers or home stores. However, many art supply stores offer pieces framed out for painting projects, and these work wonderfully for this project.

Sea glass is a lovely addition to a mosaic, but it's relatively difficult to find and can be expensive to buy. We solved that problem by creating our own, which gave us more colors than the limited choices of brown and green typically available in stores. The green, red, and cobalt blue glass is from brands of water available at most grocery stores.

In addition to free-form projects, such as the one shown here, you can combine the techniques from the original floor mosaic project (pages 70 through 73) with the ones shown here to create a different type of mosaic.

How to Create a Mosaic Wall-hanging

Tools & Materials ▶

Safety glasses	Tile
Rubber mallet	Old dishes
Tile nippers	Glass bottles
Rock tumbler	Tile mastic
Square trowel	Artist's Masonite
Grout float	Grout
Grout sponge	Cloth

Sort through the materials you've collected and decide what to use. Wearing safety glasses, put tile, dishes, or bottles inside a heavy-duty paper bag and hit them with a rubber mallet. Use tile nippers to tailor china or tile pieces, as necessary.

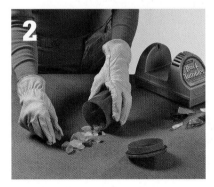

Following manufacturer's directions, tumble pieces of glass in a rock tumbler to smooth the edges and give them the look of sea glass. *Note: It will take several days to create an appreciable amount of tumbled glass.*

Draw reference lines on the Masonite and spread tile mastic on one section, using a square trowel. Embed the glass, tile, and other materials, in the mastic on that section. Continue working in small sections until the Masonite is covered.

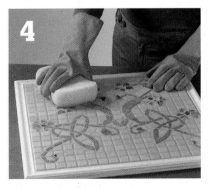

Mix a small batch of grout and spread it over the surface of the mosaic. Let the mosaic dry a few minutes, then wipe the surface with a damp grout sponge. Let the mosaic dry, then buff away any grout film with a clean, dry cloth.

Building a Tiled Sink Base

From its treadle sewing machine base to its handmade tile and hand-thrown sink, this project is unique. Other versions could be made with commercially available tile and one of the many bowl-type sinks on the market.

It isn't necessary to use a sewing machine stand, either. Many interesting or vintage pieces will work for the base. Don't destroy a valuable antique—instead, look for a stand with no top or a small chest with a badly damaged top. You'll need to remove the top anyway in order to add a plywood and cementboard core that can stand up to daily exposure to water.

After you choose a base, select a bowl-type sink basin and a specially-designed faucet, either wall- or counter-mounted. You'll need to tile the wall around a wall-mounted faucet; you'll need to make cutouts for a counter-mounted faucet. Even with a counter-mounted faucet such as the one shown here, you may want to add a small backsplash (see page 106).

If you don't like the idea of raw plywood being visible from beneath the sink, paint one side (the bottom) of the plywood before beginning to assemble the core. Coordinate the paint color with the tile and sink, so your project looks attractive from any angle.

Tools & Materials ▸

Circular saw
Drill and hole saw
Jigsaw
Utility knife
Heavy-duty stapler
Putty knife
Framing square
Trowel
Grout float
Grout sponge
Foam brush
Caulk gun
Tape measure
¾" exterior-grade
   plywood
4-mil plastic sheeting

Packing tape
½" cementboard
1½" cementboard
   screws
Fiberglass mesh
Thinset mortar
Tile
Grout and
   latex additive
Caulk
Salvaged base
Bowl-type sink basin
Faucet
Drain hardware
L-brackets

How to Make a Tiled Sink Base

Measure the base and the sink and determine a size for the plywood core. Cut the core to size.

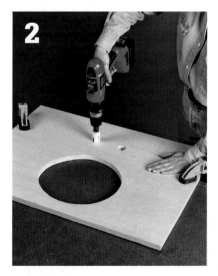

Mark a cutout for the sink on the plywood. Drill entrance holes, then use a jigsaw to make the cutout. Use the template supplied with the faucet to mark those cutouts. Use a hole saw to make the faucet cutouts.

Cut cementboard to match the dimensions of the plywood core, then use the plywood as a template to mark the cutouts on the cementboard.

(continued)

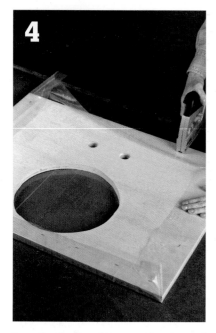

Lay plastic sheeting over the plywood core, draping it over the edges. Tack the plastic in place with staples. If you use more than one piece, overlap the seams by 6" and seal them with packing tape.

Set the plywood core on top of the base and attach it with screws driven through the base and into the core. Use angle iron or L-brackets if necessary with the base you've selected. Make sure the screws don't go through the top of the plywood.

Position the cementboard (rough-side up) on the core and attach it with 1½" screws. Make sure the screwheads are flush with the surface. Cut 1¼"-wide cementboard strips and attach them to the edges of the core with screws.

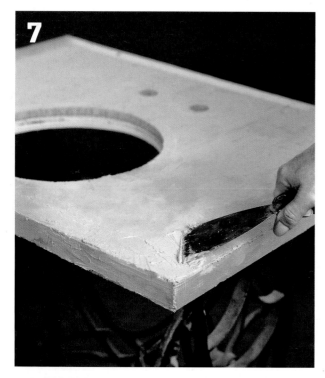

Tape all joints with fiberglass mesh. Apply three layers of tape along the edge where the top meets the edging. Fill all gaps and cover all of the tape with a layer of thinset mortar. Feather out the mortar to create a smooth, flat surface.

Dry-fit tiles to find the layout, using spacers. Once the layout is established, make marks along the vertical and horizontal rows. Draw reference lines through the marks and use a framing square to make sure the lines are perpendicular.

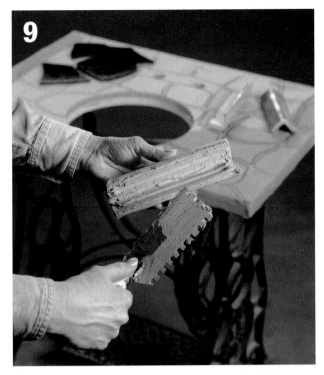

Set the edge tiles and let them dry. Install the field tiles and let them dry. Cut tile as necessary. (See pages 136 to 141 for more information on setting tile on a countertop.)

Mix a batch of grout with a latex additive and apply it with a rubber grout float. Wipe away excess grout with a damp sponge. When the grout has cured, apply sealer with a foam brush.

Apply a bead of caulk to the side of the sink, just below the lip of the ridge. Set the sink into the cutout, resting the ridge of the sink at the lip of the cutout. Make sure the joint between the sink and the counter is filled with caulk.

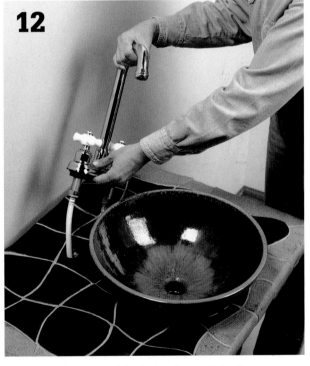

Install the faucet and drain hardware, following manufacturer's instructions.

Making Handmade Tile

Making ceramic tile from scratch is a therapeautic art for many people, requiring patience and plenty of time. The tile has to air dry for two to three weeks and then needs to be fired in a kiln twice before it's ready to be used. Before committing to the project, find a hobby shop or ceramic supply store where you can have your tile fired. Talk with the staff to find out how much the firings will cost and how long ahead they must be scheduled.

Measure the area where you plan to use the tile, and calculate how many tile you'll need for the project. It's a good idea to make more than needed to account for defective pieces. Also, be sure to check the manufacturer specifications for shrinkage (or test your chosen clay for shrinkage before committing to a large purchase). Talk with the staff at the ceramic store to figure out how much clay you'll need to produce the number of tile you need. If the tile will be used in a kitchen or near a bathroom sink, choose food-safe glazes for them.

While you're still in the exploratory phase, experiment with glazes and decorative possibilities. First, buy some low-fire clay and play with ways to make impressions. Next, buy several white or off-white matte-finish, glazed tiles. Paint glaze on the test tile in thin layers and have them fired. When you're satisfied with the results, you're ready to make your own tile.

Tools & Materials ▸

Straightedge	Blanket or bubblewrap
Utility knife	Canvas
Rolling pin	Low-fire clay
Clay squeegee	Seashells or other
Craft knife	imprinting objects
Spatula	Plywood scraps
Paintbrushes	Low-fire glazes
Stiff cardboard	Paintbrushes
Paring knife	Ruler or measuring tape

How to Make Handmade Tile

On a piece of stiff cardboard, draw a template for the tile. Measure carefully and allow for shrinkage. (For example, a 4⅝ × 4⅝-inch template should produce a 4 × 4-inch tile, factoring in a 12% shrinkage rate.) Measure diagonally from corner to corner; when the diagonals are precisely equal, the template is square. Cut out the template, using a straightedge and utility knife.

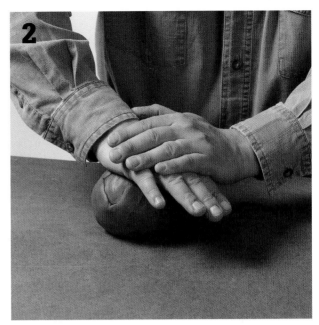

Take out a one-pound chunk of clay and pat it into a ball. Close the bag securely to keep the remaining clay from drying out. Put the clay on a smooth work surface and pound it with the palm of your hand, flattening the ball. (Don't fold the clay over itself—this traps air in the clay.)

Cover the clay with a piece of canvas. Roll out the clay to a uniform thickness. Change directions as you roll the clay so the clay particles will be evenly distributed. If all the clay particles go the same direction, the tile will shrink unevenly as it's fired. (Inset) Lay two ½" plywood scraps on the table as guides.

Dip the edge of a clean squeegee in water. Take the canvas off the clay and pull the squeegee across the clay, smoothing the surface. Work in one direction only, and rinse the squeegee as often as necessary to keep the edge clean.

(continued)

5

Carefully place the template on the clay. Holding it firmly against the clay with one hand, use the utility knife to cut around the template. Pull the extra clay away from the tile and run the knife around the edges again.

6

Scoot the tile to the side to make sure it's not stuck to the work surface. Wet your index finger and use it to smooth the corners and sides of the tile. Gently press a clean shell into the clay to create the desired design.

7

Pick up the tile with a spatula and set it on a scrap of plywood to dry. If the tile has gotten distorted, nudge it back into shape.

8

Continue cutting out tile. Set them out of direct sunlight to dry.

Let the tiles dry for a day or two, until they're dried to the consistency of leather. Using a paring knife, trim any bulging edges. Allow the tiles to dry completely, which should take two to three weeks. If the air is extremely dry, the tile may dry too quickly. Lay a cloth over them to slow down the drying process.

Put the tiles on a sturdy tray or piece of flat plywood and wrap it in a blanket or bubble wrap. Carefully transport the dried tile to a kiln for a bisque firing.

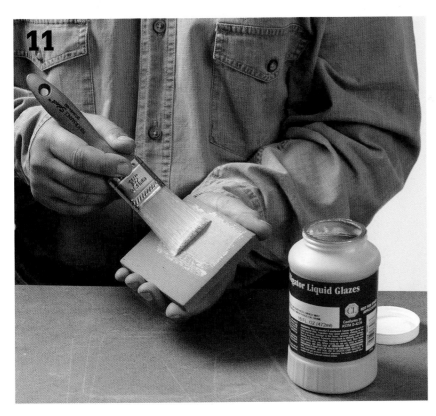

Brush two or three thin coats of glaze onto the fired (and already cool) tile. Let the glaze dry to touch between coats. Have the tile fired a second and final time.

Outdoor Projects

Tile makes as much sense in your outdoor home as it does indoors. Its durability, ease of maintenance, and attractive appearance brings good things to patios, gardens, and outdoor kitchens, to name just a few places.

In This Chapter:

- Tiling Concrete Steps
- Tiling a Patio Slab
- Building a Tiled Garden Bench

A long, spare table covered in bright blue tile makes an effective counterpoint to the neutral quarry tile floor and natural stone walls.

In this alcove, decorative tiles grace a fireplace surround topped by a brick mantel. The floor combines large quarry tile with interesting accent tiles that emphasize the Mediterranean feeling of the patio. Accessories scattered throughout the area echo the blue-and-white theme set by the fireplace and accent tiles.

A tiled fountain nestles into a flagstone patio, adding a welcome spot of color to the landscape in every season.

This raised patio floor is adorned with porcelain tile in a variety of sizes and shapes. The colors and textures of the tiles complement other elements of the scene, including the stone wall, the terra-cotta planters, and the weathered wood chair.

Variegated blue tile set on the diagonal transform a simple rectangular hot tub into something of an oasis in this backyard landscape.

The texture and mottled colors in this beautiful tile take a broad expanse of walkway far beyond its utilitarian purpose.

Nothing more than two colors of plain rectangular tile, but this distinctive herringbone pattern produces the aura of sunshine and sea breezes.

The golden color of this home's exterior is reflected in the mottled colors of the tile patio and accented by the sunny yellow patio furniture.

Each riser outfitted with its own design, this tiled staircase becomes an Italian-style showcase.

The textured surface and alternating shapes and patterns of these warm colored ceramic tiles evoke the feeling of a wooden deck.

This dining area is defined by the rug-like effect of a design area set into a border of larger tile set on the diagonal.

Tiling Concrete Steps

In addition to the traditional tricks for improving your home's curb appeal—landscaping, fresh paint, pretty windows—a tiled entry makes a wonderful, positive impression. To be suitable for tiling, stair treads must be deep enough to walk on safely. Check local building codes for specifics, but most require that treads be at least 11" deep (from front to back) after the tile is added.

Before you start laying any tiles, the concrete must be free of curing agents, clean, and in good shape. Make necessary repairs and give them time to cure. An isolation membrane can be applied before the tile. This membrane can be a fiberglass sheet or it can be brushed on as a liquid to dry. In either case, it separates the tile from the concrete, which allows the two to move independently and protects the tile from potential settling or shifting of the concrete.

Choose exterior-rated, unglazed floor tile with a skid-resistant surface. Tile for the walking surfaces should be at least ½" thick. Use bullnose tiles at the front edges of treads (as you would on a countertop) and use cove tiles as the bottom course on risers.

Tools & Materials ▸

Pressure washer
Masonry trowel
4-foot level
Carpenter's square
Straightedge
Tape measure
Chalk line
Tile cutter or wet saw
Tile nippers
Square-notched
  trowel
Needle-nose plier
Rubber mallet
Grout float
Grout sponge
Caulk gun
Latex or epoxy
  patching
  compound
Isolation membrane

Tile spacers
Buckets
Paintbrush and roller
Plastic sheeting
Paper towels
Dry-set mortar
Field tile
Bullnose tile
Grout
Grout additive
Latex tile caulk
Grout sealer
Tile sealer
2 × 4
Carpet scrap
Cold chisel or
  flat-head
  screwdriver
Wire brush
Broom

How to Tile Concrete Steps

Use a pressure washer to clean the surface of the concrete. (Use a washer with at least 4,000 psi and follow manufacturer's instructions carefully to avoid damaging the concrete with the pressurized spray.)

Dig out rubble in large cracks and chips, using a small cold chisel or flat-head screwdriver. Use a wire brush to loosen dirt and debris in small cracks. Sweep the area or use a wet/dry vacuum to remove all debris.

Fill small cracks and chips with masonry patching compound, using a masonry trowel. Allow the patching compound to cure according to manufacturer's directions.

If damage is located at a front edge, clean it as described above. Place a board in front and block the board in place with bricks or concrete blocks. Wet the damaged area and fill it with patching compound. Use a masonry trowel to smooth the patch and then allow it to cure thoroughly.

Test the surface of the steps and stoop for low spots, using a 4-foot level or other straightedge. Fill any low spots with patching compound and allow the compound to cure thoroughly.

(continued)

Spread a layer of isolation membrane over the concrete, using a notched trowel. Smooth the surface of the membrane, using the flat edge of a trowel. Allow the membrane to cure according to manufacturer's directions.

The sequence is important when tiling a stairway with landing. The primary objective is to install the tile in such a way that the fewest possible cut edges are visible from the main viewing position. If you are tiling the sides of concrete steps, start laying tile there first. Begin by extending horizontal lines from the tops of the stair treads back to the house on the sides of the steps. Use a 4-foot level.

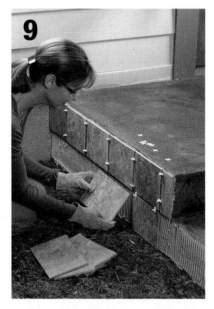

Mix a batch of thinset mortar with latex bonding adhesive and trowel it onto the sides of the steps, trying to retain visibility of the layout lines. Because the top steps are likely more visible than the bottom steps, start on top and work your way down.

Begin setting tiles into the thinset mortar on the sides of the steps. Start at the top and work your way downward. Try to lay out tile so the vertical gaps between tiles align. Use spacers if you need to.

Wrap a 2 × 4 in old carpet and drag it back and forth across the tile surfaces to set them evenly. Don't get too aggressive here—you don't want to dislodge all of the thinset mortar.

Measure the width of a riser, including the thickness of the tiles you've laid on the step sides. Calculate the centerpoint and mark it clearly with chalk or a high visibility marker.

Next, install the tiles on the stair risers. Because the location of the tops of the riser tiles affects the positioning of the tread and landing tiles, you'll get the most accurate layout if the riser tiles are laid first. Start by stacking tiles vertically against the riser. (In some cases, you'll only need one tile to reach from tread to tread.) Add spacers. Trace the location of the tread across the back of the top tile to mark it for cutting.

Cut enough tiles to size to lay tiles for all the stair risers. Be sure to allow enough space for grout joints if you are stacking tiles.

Trowel thinset mortar mixed with bonding adhesive onto the faces of the risers. In most cases, you should be able to tile each riser all at once.

Lay tiles on the risers. The bottom tile edges can rest on the tread, and the tops of the top tiles should be flush with or slightly lower than the plane of the tread above.

(continued)

Dry-lay tile in both directions on the stair landing. You'll want to maintain the same grout lines that are established by the riser tiles, but you'll want to evaluate the front-to-back layout to make sure you don't end up with a row of tiles that is less than 2" or so in thickness.

Cut tiles as indicated by your dry run, and then begin installing them by troweling thinset adhesive for the bullnose tiles at the front edge of the landing. The tiles should overlap the top edges of the riser tiles, but not extend past their faces.

Field tile

Bullnose tile

Set the first row of field tiles, maintaining an even gap between the field tiles and the bullnose tiles.

Add the last row of tiles next to the house and threshold, cutting them as needed so they are between ¼" and ½" away from the house.

20

Install tiles on the stair treads, starting at the top tread and working your way downward. Set a bullnose tile on each side of the centerline and work your way toward the sides, making sure to conceal the step side tiles with the tread tiles.

21

Fill in the field tiles on the stair treads, being sure to leave a gap between the back tiles and the riser tiles that's the same thickness as the other tile gaps.

22

Let the thinset mortar cure for a few days, and then apply grout in the gaps between tiles using a grout float. Wipe away the grout after it clouds over. Cover with plastic, in the event of rain.

23

After a few weeks, seal the grout lines with an exterior-rated grout sealer.

24

Select (or have prepared) a pretinted caulk that's the same color as your grout. Fill the gap between the back row of tiles and the house with caulk. Smooth with a wet finger if needed.

Tiling a Patio Slab

Outdoor tile can be made of several different materials and is available in many colors and styles. A popular current trend is to use natural stone tiles with different shapes and complementary colors, as demonstrated in this project. Tile manufacturers may offer brochures giving you ideas for modular patterns that can be created from their tiles. Make sure the tiles you select are intended for outdoor use.

When laying a modular, geometric pattern with tiles of different sizes, it's crucial that you test the layout before you begin and that you place the first tiles very carefully. The first tiles will dictate the placement of all other tiles in your layout.

You can pour a new masonry slab on which to install your tile patio, but another option is to finish an existing slab by veneering it with tile—the scenario demonstrated here.

Outdoor tile must be installed on a clean, flat, and stable surface. When tiling an existing concrete pad, the surface must be free of flaking, wide cracks, and other major imperfections. A damaged slab can be repaired by applying a 1- to 2"-thick layer of new concrete over the old surface before laying tile.

Note: Wear eye protection when cutting tile and handle cut tiles carefully—the cut edges of some materials may be very sharp.

Tools & Materials ▶

Tape measure	Caulk gun
Pencil	Tile spacers
Chalk line	Buckets
Tile cutter or wet saw	Paintbrush and roller
Tile nippers	Plastic sheeting
Square-notched trowel	Thinset mortar
2 × 4 padded with	Modular tile
carpet	Grout
Hammer	Grout additive
Grout float	Grout sealer
Grout sponge	Tile sealer
Cloth	Foam brush

Materials & Tools for Landscape Installations

Tile options for landscape installations: Slate and other smooth, natural stone materials are durable and blend well with any landscape but are usually expensive. Quarry tile is less expensive, though only available in limited colors. Exterior-rated porcelain or ceramic tiles are moderately priced and available in a wide range of colors and textures, with many styles imitating the look of natural stone. Terra-cotta tile is made from molded clay for use in warmer, drier climates only. Many of these materials require application of a sealer to increase durability and prevent staining and moisture penetration.

Tools for installing exterior tile include: a wet saw for cutting tile quickly and easily (available at rental centers—make certain to rent one that is big enough for the tile size you install), an angle grinder with a diamond-edged cutting blade (also a rental item) for cutting curves or other complex contours, a trowel with square notches (of the size required for your tile size) for spreading the mortar adhesive, spacers for accurate aligning of tiles and setting consistent joint widths, a straight length of 2 × 4 padded along one edge (carpet pad works well) for helping align tile surfaces, a grout float for spreading grout to fill the joints, and a sponge for cleaning excess grout from tile surfaces.

Materials for installing exterior tile include: latex-modified thinset mortar adhesive that is mixed with water (if you can't find thinset that is latex modified, buy unmodified thinset and mix it with a latex additive for mortar, following manufacturer's directions), exterior-rated grout available in a variety of colors to match the tile you use, grout additive to improve durability, grout sealer to help protect grout from moisture and staining, and tile sealer required for some tile materials (follow tile manufacturer's requirements).

Slate

Cut stone

Terra-cotta tile

Quarry tile

Ceramic tile

(continued)

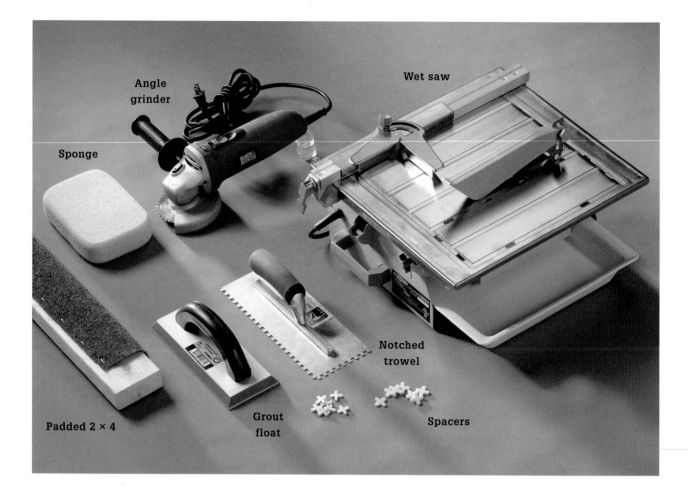

Angle grinder

Wet saw

Sponge

Notched trowel

Padded 2 × 4

Grout float

Spacers

Thinset mortar

Grout

Grout sealers

Grout additive

How to Tile a Patio Slab

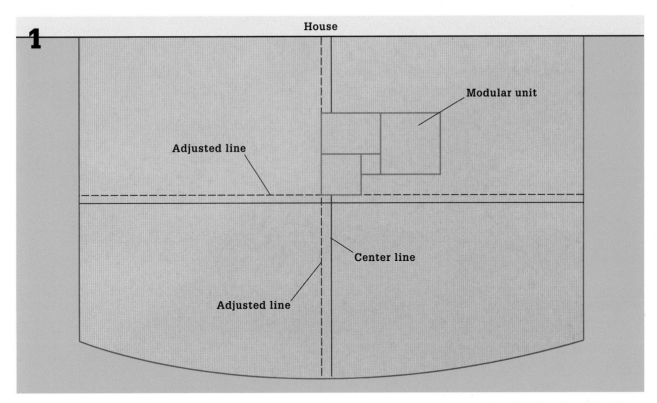

To establish a layout for tile with a modular pattern, you must carefully determine the location of the first tile. On the clean and dry concrete surface, measure and mark a centerline down the center of the slab. Test-fit tiles along the line—because of the modular pattern used here, the tiles are staggered. Mark the edge of a tile nearest the center of the pad, then create a second line perpendicular to the first and test-fit tiles along this line.

Make adjustments as needed so the modular pattern breaks evenly over the patio surface, and is symetrical from side to side. You may need to adjust the position of one or both lines. The intersection of the lines is where your tile installation will begin. Outline the position of each group of tiles on the slab.

(continued)

Variation: To establish a traditional grid pattern, test-fit rows of tiles so they run in each direction, intersecting at the center of the patio. Adjust the layout to minimize tile cutting at the sides and ends, then mark the final layout and snap chalklines across the patio to create four quadrants. As you lay tile, work along the chalklines and in one quadrant at a time.

Following manufacturer's instructions, mix enough thinset mortar to work for about 2 hours (start with 4 to 5" deep in a 5-gallon bucket. At the intersection of the two layout lines, use a notched-edge trowel to spread thinset mortar over an area large enough to accommodate the layout of the first modular group of tiles. Hold the trowel at a 45° angle to rake the mortar to a consistent depth.

Set the first tile, twisting it slightly as you push it into the mortar. Align it with both adjusted layout lines, then place a padded 2 × 4 over the center of the tile and give it a light rap with a hammer to set the tile.

Position the second tile adjacent to the first with a slight gap between them. Place spacers on end in the joint near each corner and push the second tile against the spacers. Make certain the first tile remains aligned with the layout lines. Set the padded 2 × 4 across both tiles and tap to set. Use a damp cloth to remove any mortar that squeezes out of the joint or gets on tile surfaces. Joints must be at least ⅛"-deep to hold grout.

Lay the remaining tiles of the first modular unit, using spacers. Using the trowel, scrape the excess mortar from the concrete pad in areas you will not yet be working to prevent it from hardening and interfering with tile installation.

With the first modular unit set, continue laying tile following the pattern established. You can use the chalklines for general reference, but they will not be necessary as layout lines. To prevent squeeze-out between tiles, scrape a heavy accumulation of mortar ½" away from the edge of a set tile before setting the adjacent tile.

Tip: Cutting Contours in Tile ▸

To make convex (left) or concave (right) curves, mark the profile of the curve on the tile, then use a wet saw to make parallel straight cuts, each time cutting as close to the marked line as possible. Use a tile nippers to break off small portions of tabs, gradually working down to the curve profile. Finally, use an angle grinder to smooth off the sharp edges of the tabs. Make sure to wear a particle mask when using the tile saw and wear sturdy gloves when using the nippers.

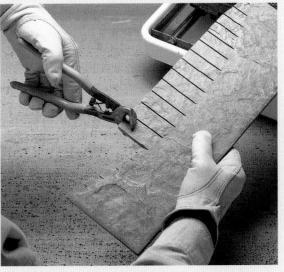

(continued)

After installing the tile, remove all the spacers, cover the tiled area with plastic, and let the thinset mortar cure according to the manufacturer's instructions. When tile has fully set, remove the plastic and mix grout, using a grout additive instead of water. Grout additive is especially important in outdoor applications, because it creates joints that are more resilient in changing temperatures.

Use a grout float to spread grout over an area that is roughly 10 sq. ft. Push down with the face of the float to force grout into the joints, then hold the float edge at a 45° angle to the tile surfaces and scrape off the excess grout.

Once you've grouted this area, wipe off the grout residue, using a damp sponge. Wipe with a light, circular motion—you want to clean tile surfaces but not pull grout out of the joints. Don't try to get the tile perfectly clean the first time. Wipe the area several times, rinsing out the sponge frequently.

11

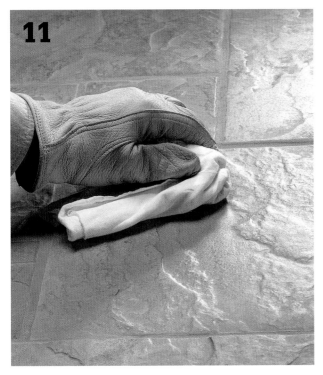

Once the grout has begun to set (usually about 1 hour, depending on temperature and humidity), clean the tile surfaces again. You want to thoroughly clean grout residue from tile surfaces because it is difficult to remove once it has hardened. Buff off a light film left after final cleaning with a cloth.

Grouting Porous Tiles ▸

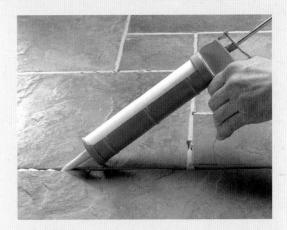

Some tiles, such as slate, have highly porous surfaces that can be badly stained by grout. For these tiles, apply grout by filling an empty caulk tube (available at tile stores and some building centers) with grout, and apply the grout to the joints with a caulk gun. Cut the tip to make an opening just large enough to allow grout to be forced out. Run the tip down the joint between tiles as you squeeze out the grout. Remove the grout that gets on the tile surface with a wet sponge. You may need to use your finger to force grout into the joint—protect your skin by wearing a heavy glove to do this.

12

Cover the pad with plastic and let the grout cure according to manufacturer's instructions. Once the grout has cured, use a foam brush to apply grout sealer to only the grout, wiping any spillover off of tile surfaces.

13

Apply tile sealer to the entire surface, using a paint roller. Cover the patio with plastic and allow the sealer to dry completely before exposing the patio to weather or traffic.

Building a Tiled Garden Bench

Here's a splendid example of the term "return on investment." Four decorative tiles and a handful of coordinated accent tiles produce quite an impact. In fact, those accents and a few dozen 4 × 4" tiles transform a plain cedar bench into a special garden ornament. And you can accomplish the whole thing over one weekend.

Tools

Tape measure
Circular saw
Drill
Stapler
Power or hand
    miter saw (optional)
Utility knife
Chalk line
Cloth
¼" notched trowel
Needlenose pliers
Grout float
Sponge
Notched trowel

Materials

2 cedar 2 × 4s (8 ft.)
1 cedar 2 × 6 (8 ft.)
1 cedar 4 × 4 (8 ft.)
4 × 4 ft. sheet of
    ¾" exterior plywood
4 × 4 ft. sheet of
    ½" cementboard
Plastic sheeting
2" galvanized deck screws
3" galvanized deck screws
1¼" cementboard screws
Clear sealer
Field and accent tile
Thinset mortar
Tile spacers
Grout
Grout sealer
150-grit sandpaper

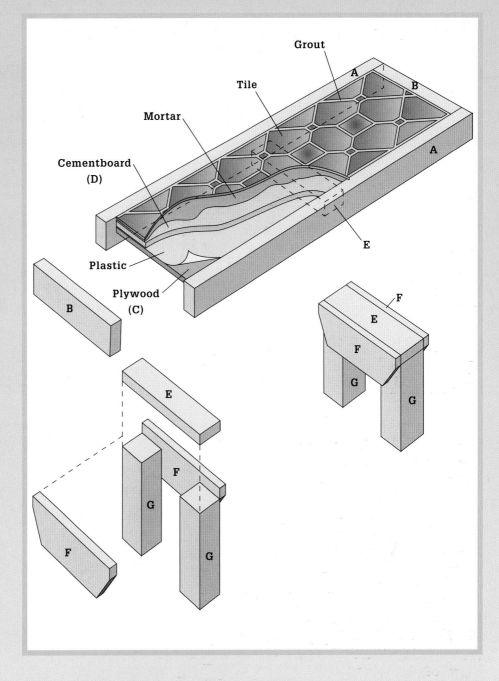

Cutting List

Key	Part	Dimension	Pcs.	Material
A	Sides	1½ × 3½ × 51"	2	Cedar
B	Ends	1½ × 3½ × 16"	2	Cedar
C	Core	15 × 48"	1	Ext. Plywood
D	Core	15 × 48"	1	Cementboard
E	Stretchers	1½ × 3½ × 16"	3	Cedar
F	Braces	1½ × 5½ × 16"	4	Cedar
G	Legs	3½ × 3½ × 13"	4	Cedar

How to Build a Tiled Garden Bench

Cut two sides and two ends, then position the ends between the sides so the edges are flush. Make sure the frame is square. Drill ⅛" pilot holes through the sides and into the ends. Drive 3" screws through the pilot holes.

Cut three stretchers. Mark the sides, 4½" from the inside of each end. Using 1½" blocks beneath them as spacers, position the stretchers and make sure they're level. Drill pilot holes and fasten the stretchers to the sides with 3" screws.

Cut one 15 × 48" core from ¾" exterior-grade plywood and another the same size from cementboard. Staple plastic sheeting over the plywood, draping it over the edges. Lay the cementboard rough-side up on the plywood and attach it with 1¼" cementboard screws driven every 6". Make sure the screw heads are flush with the surface.

4

Position the bench frame upside down and over the plywood/cementboard core. Drill pilot holes and then drive 2" galvanized deck screws through the stretchers and into the plywood.

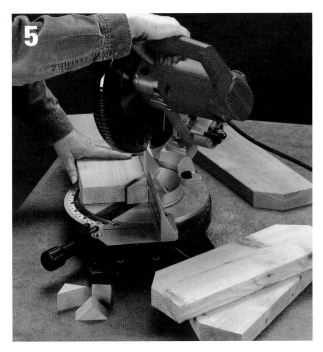

5

Cut four braces from a cedar 2 × 6. Mark the angle on each end of each brace by measuring down 1½" from the top edge and 1½" along the bottom edge. Draw a line between the two points and cut along that line, using a power or hand miter saw or a circular saw.

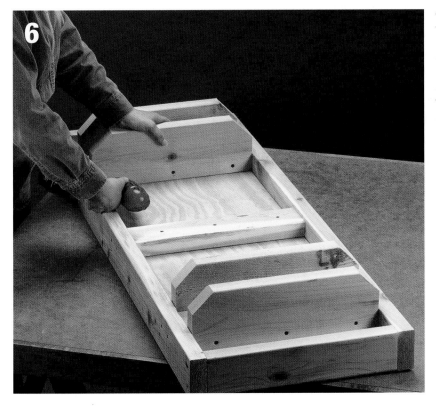

6

On each brace, measure down ¾" from the top edge and draw a reference line across the stretcher for the screw positions. Drill ⅛" pilot holes along the reference line. Position a brace on each side of the end stretchers and fasten them with 3" screws driven through the braces and into the stretchers.

(continued)

7

Cut four 13" legs from a 4 × 4. Position each leg between a set of braces and against the sides of the bench frame. Drill pilot holes through each brace and attach the leg to the braces by driving 3" screws through the braces and into the leg. Repeat the process for each leg. Sand all surfaces with 150-grit sandpaper, then seal all wood surfaces with clear wood sealer.

8

Snap perpendicular reference lines to mark the center of the length and width of the bench. Beginning at the center of the bench, dry-fit the field tiles, include spacers. Set the accent tile in place and mark the field tile for cutting.

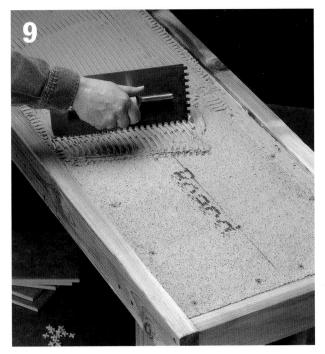

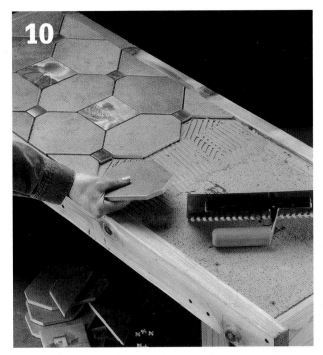

Cut the field tile and continue dry-fitting the bench top, including the accent and border tiles. When you're satisfied, remove the tile and apply thinset mortar over the cementboard, using a notched trowel.

Set the tile into the thinset mortar, using a slight twisting motion. Continue adding thinset and setting the tile until the bench top is covered. Remove the spacers. Let the mortar dry according to manufacturer's directions. (See pages 56 to 63 for more information on setting tile.)

Mix grout and use a grout float to force it into the joints surrounding the tile. Wipe excess grout away with a damp sponge. When the grout has dried slightly, polish the tiles with a clean, dry cloth to remove the slight haze of grout. (See page 60 for more information on grouting tile.)

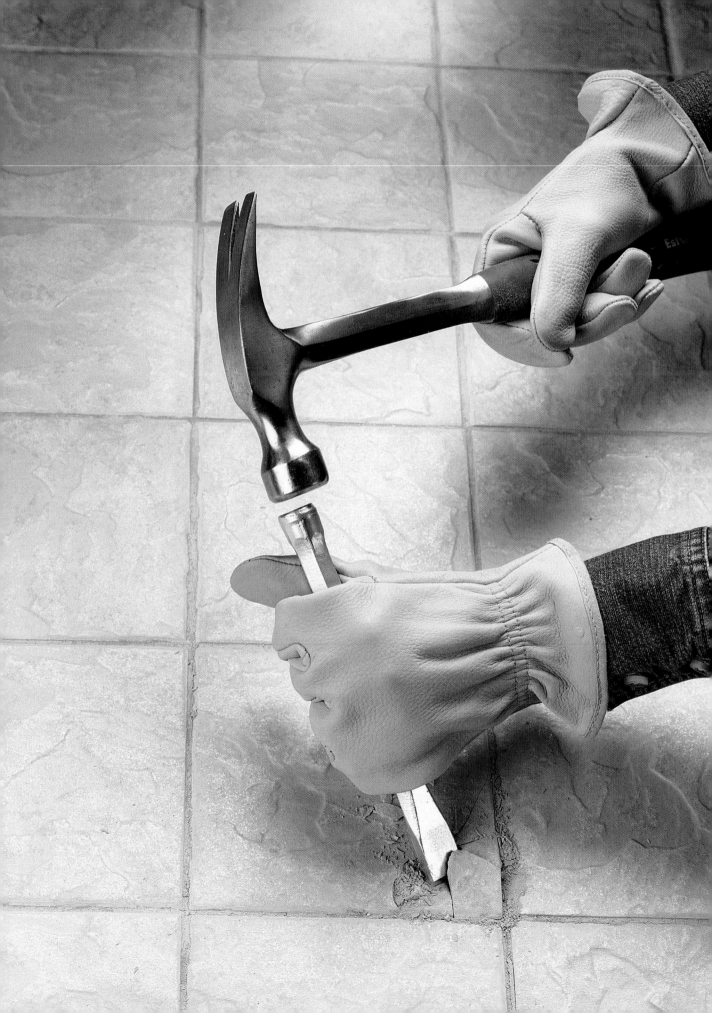

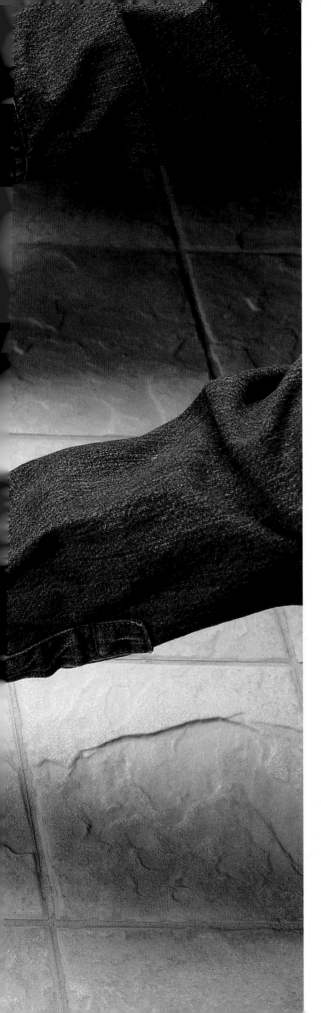

Repair Projects

Tile is extremely durable, but like any other construction material, it requires maintenance and occasional repairs. This chapter leads you through the most common repair projects: replacing grout, removing and replacing a broken tile, and replacing accessories, such as a ceramic soap dish.

When it comes to tile, replacing grout is the most common repair project because the grout is the most vulnerable part of the installation. While a small crack or hole in a grout joint may not seem like a major issue, in floors and wet walls it allows water to seep behind the tile and can lead to serious damage over time. Like any other repair, taking care of grout issues while they're small prevents much larger problems later. This chapter gives you all the information you'll need to take excellent care of all your floor tile, wall tile, and its grout.

In This Chapter:

- Maintaining Wall Tile
- Maintaining Floor Tile

Maintaining Wall Tile

As we've said throughout this book, ceramic tile is durable and nearly maintenance-free, but like every other material in your house, it can fail or develop problems. The most common problem with ceramic tile involves damaged grout. Failed grout is unattractive, but the real danger is that it offers a point of entry for water. Given a chance to work its way beneath grout, water can destroy a tile base and eventually wreck an entire installation. It's important to regrout ceramic tile as soon as you see signs of damage.

Another potential problem for tile installations is damaged caulk. In tub and shower stalls and around sinks and backsplashes, the joints between the tile and the fixtures are sealed with caulk. The caulk eventually deteriorates, leaving an entry point for water. Unless the joints are recaulked, seeping water will destroy the tile base and the wall.

In bathrooms, towel rods, soap dishes, and other accessories can work loose from walls, especially if they weren't installed correctly or aren't supported properly. For maximum holding power, anchor new accessories to wall studs or blocking. If no studs or blocking are available, use special fasteners, such as toggle bolts or molly bolts, to anchor the accessories directly to the surface of the underlying wall. To hold screws firmly in place in ceramic tile walls, drill pilot holes and insert plastic sleeves, which expand when screws are driven into them.

Tools & Materials ▶

Awl	Tile adhesive
Utility knife	Masking tape
Trowel	Grout
Grout float	Cloth or rag
Hammer	Rubbing alcohol
Chisel	Mildew remover
Small pry bar	Silicone or latex caulk
Eye protection	Sealer
Replacement tile	Sponge

How to Regrout Wall Tile

Use an awl or utility knife to scrape out the old grout completely, leaving a clean bed for the new grout.

Clean and rinse the grout joints, then spread grout over the entire tile surface, using a rubber grout float or sponge. Work the grout well into the joints and let it set slightly.

Wipe away excess grout with a damp sponge. When the grout is dry, wipe away the residue and polish the tiles with a dry cloth.

How to Recaulk a Joint

Start with a completely dry surface. Scrape out the old caulk and clean the joint with a cloth dipped in rubbing alcohol. If this is a bathtub or sink, fill it with water to weigh it down.

Clean the joint with a product that kills mildew spores; let it dry. Fill the joint with silicone or latex caulk.

Wet your fingertip with cold water, then use your finger to smooth the caulk into a cove shape. After the caulk hardens, use a utility knife to trim away any excess.

How to Replace Built-in Wall Accessories

Carefully remove the damaged accessory (see page 242). Scrape away any remaining adhesive or grout. Apply dry-set tile adhesive to the back side of the new accessory, then press it firmly in place.

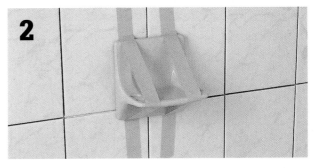

Use masking tape to hold the accessory in place while the adhesive dries. Let the mortar dry completely (12 to 24 hours), then grout and seal the area.

How to Replace Surface-mounted Accessories

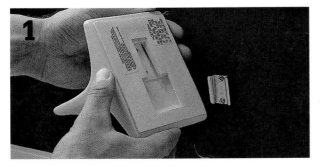

Lift the accessory up and off the mounting plate. If the mounting plate screws are driven into studs or blocking, simply hang the new accessory. If not, add hardware such as molly bolts, toggle bolts, or plastic anchor sleeves.

Put a dab of silicone caulk over the pilot holes and the tips of the screws before inserting them. Let the caulk dry, then install the new fixture on the mounting plate.

How to Remove & Replace Broken Wall Tiles

Carefully scrape away the grout from the surrounding joints, using a utility knife or an awl. Break the damaged tile into small pieces, using a hammer and chisel. Remove the broken pieces, then scrape away debris or old adhesive from the open area.

If the tile to be replaced is a cut tile, cut a new one to match (see page 254). Test-fit the new tile and make sure it sits flush with the field. Spread adhesive on the back of the replacement tile and place it in the hole, twisting it slightly. Use masking tape to hold the tile in place for 24 hours so the adhesive can dry.

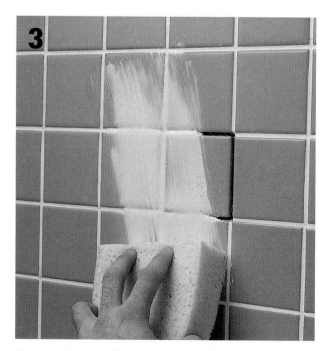

Remove the tape, then apply premixed grout, using a sponge or grout float. Let the grout set slightly, then tool it with a rounded object such as a toothbrush handle. Wipe away excess grout with a damp cloth.

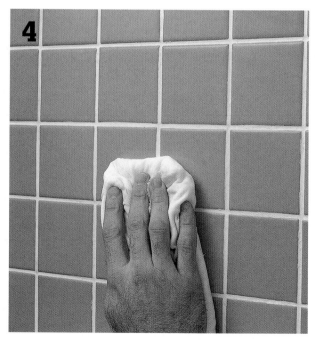

Let the grout dry for an hour, then polish the tile with a clean, dry cloth.

Maintaining Floor Tile

Tile floors are extremely durable, but they do require periodic maintenance. Accidents happen and although it takes quite an impact to break a floor tile, it is possible. Broken tile or failed grout can expose the underlayment to moisture which will destroy the floor in time.

Major cracks in grout joints indicate that movement of the floor has caused the adhesive layer beneath the tile to deteriorate. The adhesive layer must be replaced along with the grout in order to create a permanent repair.

Perhaps the biggest challenge with tile repair is matching the grout color. If you're regrouting an entire floor, just select the color that complements the tile; if you're replacing a tile, you have to blend the new grout with the old.

A good tile dealer can help you get the best color match.

Any time you remove tile, check the underlayment. If it's no longer smooth, solid, and level, repair or replace it before repairing the tile.

Protect unglazed tile from stains and water spots by periodically applying a coat of tile sealer. Keep dirt from getting trapped in grout lines by sealing them every year or two.

How to Regrout a Ceramic Tile Floor

Completely remove the old grout, using a rotary tool, utility knife (and several blades), or a grout saw. Spread the new grout over the tiles, using a rubber grout float. Force grout into the joints, holding the float almost flat, then drag the float across the joints diagonally, tilting the face at a 45° angle.

Remove excess grout by making a second pass with the float. Work diagonally across the joint lines, and tilt the float at a steep angle to the tile faces.

Let the grout set for 10 to 15 minutes, then wipe away excess with a damp sponge, rinsing frequently. Fill in low spots by applying and smoothing extra grout with your finger. Let the grout dry for about an hour, then polish the tile faces with a dry cloth to remove the powdery residue. Seal the grout after it cures completely.

How to Replace a Floor Tile

Remove the grout from around the damaged tile, using a rotary tool, utility knife (and several blades), or a grout saw. Then, carefully break apart the tile, using a cold chisel and hammer.

Scrape away the old adhesive with a putty knife. Make sure the base surface is smooth and flat.

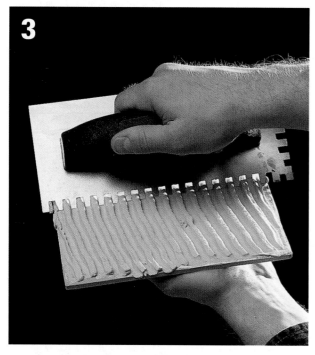

Use a notched trowel to cover the entire back of the replacement tile with an even layer of thinset mortar.

Set the tile in place, and press down firmly to create a good bond. If necessary, use a carpet-covered 2 × 4 and a rubber mallet to tap the tile flush with the neighboring tiles.

5

Use a small screwdriver to remove excess mortar that has oozed into the grout joints, then wipe up any mortar from the tile surface. When the mortar has dried completely, grout around the tile (page 60).

Maintaining Grout ▶

Like the tile on your bathroom or kitchen walls, floor tile must be watertight. All the grout lines must be solid and full, and every tile must be free of cracks or chips. Neglecting problems can result in damage to the underlayment and subfloor, and possibly to the entire tile job.

Perhaps the greatest challenge with tile repair is matching the grout color. If you're regrouting an entire floor, just select a color that complements the tile; if you're replacing a tile, you have to blend the new grout with the old. A good tile dealer can help you get the best color match.

Tools & Materials

This chapter describes and illustrates the tools and materials necessary for the tile projects presented throughout the book. Most homeowners, especially those who enjoy do-it-yourself projects, already own many of the tools and materials necessary for tile projects. From the saws and flat bars necessary for removing old surfaces to the drills and utility knives handy for repairing and installing substrates, many are basic components of a standard toolkit. Others, such as a snap cutter, are not common, but neither are they expensive or difficult to use.

There are a few less common and more expensive tools that, while not strictly necessary, will simplify large projects to such a degree that you may want to add them to your arsenal. A tile wet saw, for example, cuts even heavy tile easily and simplifies tricky cuts. For small projects you may want to rent a tile saw; for large projects you may want to purchase the saw.

Materials for tile projects range from cementboard to cork, from thinset mastic to grout. These materials are widely available and reasonably priced. The important issue is matching the product to the project. This chapter will help you do exactly that.

In This Chapter:

- Tools for Removing Old Surfaces
- Tools for Repairing & Installing Substrates
- Tools for Installing Substrates
- Tools for Layout
- Tools for Cutting Tile
- Tools for Setting & Grouting Tile
- Preparation Materials
- Materials for Setting & Grouting Tile

Tools for Removing Old Surfaces

Quality tools remove old surfaces faster and leave surfaces ready to accept new tile. Home centers and hardware stores carry a variety of products for surface removal. Look for tools with smooth, secure handles and correctly weighted heads for safety and comfort.

End-cutting nippers allow you to pull out staples remaining in the floor after carpeting is removed. This plier-like tool can also be used to break an edge on old tile so a chisel or pry bar can be inserted.

Heat guns are used to soften adhesives so vinyl base cove moldings and stubborn tiles can be pryed away from the wall. They are also used to remove old paint, especially when it is heavily layered or badly chipped.

Hand mauls are often used in combination with pry bars and chisels to remove old flooring and prepare surfaces for tile. They are helpful for leveling high spots on concrete floors and separating underlayments and subfloors.

Flat pry bars are used to remove wood base moldings from walls and to separate underlayments and floor coverings from subfloors. This tool is also effective for removing tiles set in mortar.

Chisels come in a variety of sizes for specific jobs. Masonry chisels are used with hand mauls to remove high spots in concrete. Cold chisels are used with hand mauls or hammers to pry tiles from mortar.

Floor scrapers are used to scrape and smooth patched areas on concrete floors and to pry up flooring, and scrape adhesives and backings from underlayments.

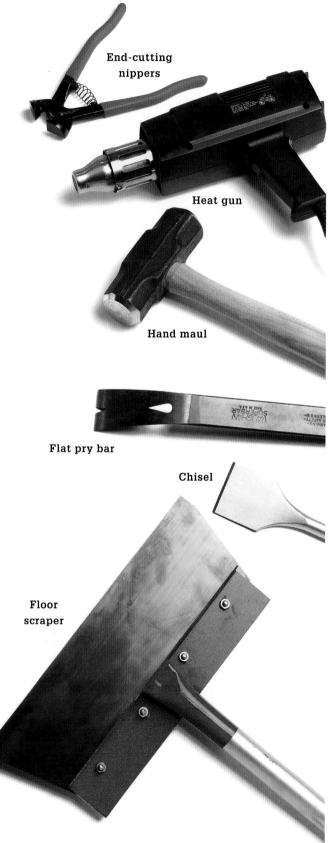

End-cutting nippers

Heat gun

Hand maul

Flat pry bar

Chisel

Floor scraper

Tools for Repairing & Installing Substrates

Surfaces and substrates must be in good condition before new tile can be installed. Use the tools below to create stiff, flat surfaces that help prevent tiles from cracking and enhance the overall appearance of your finished project.

Straightedges are used to mark damaged areas of substrate for removal. They are also used to measure and mark replacement pieces for cutting.

Jigsaws are handy when cutting notches, holes, and irregular shapes in new or existing substrates. They are also used to fit new substrate pieces to existing doorways.

Portable drills secure substrates to subfloors, with screws selected for the thickness and type of substrate used.

Circular saws are used to remove damaged sections of subfloor and cut replacement pieces to fit.

Straightedge

Portable drill

Circular saw

Jigsaw

Tools for Installing Substrates

Depending upon your application, you may have to cut and install a substrate of cementboard, plywood, cork, backerboard, greenboard, or moisture membrane. Whichever your tiling project demands, the tools shown here will help you measure, score, cut, and install substrate material with precision.

Drywall squares are used to measure and mark substrates, such as cementboard, fiber/cementboard, and isolation membrane. They can also be used as straightedge guides for scoring and cutting substrates with a utility knife.

Utility knives are usually adequate for scoring straight lines in wallboard, cementboard, fiber/cementboard, and for cutting isolation membrane substrates. However, because cementboard and fiber/cementboard are thick, hard substrates, utility knife blades must be replaced often for best performance.

Cementboard knives are the best choice for scoring cementboard and fiber/cementboard. The blades on these knives are stronger and wear better than utility knife blades when cutting rough surfaces.

Trowels are useful for applying leveler on existing floors and for applying thinset mortar to substrates. Trowels can also be used to scrape away ridges and high spots after levelers or mortars dry.

T-square

Utility knife

Cementboard knife

Notched trowel

Tools for Layout

Laying tile requires careful planning. Since tile is installed following a grid-pattern layout, marking perpendicular reference lines is essential to proper placement. Use the tools shown here to measure and mark reference lines for any type of tiling project.

Straightedges are handy for marking reference lines on small areas. They can also be used to mark cutting lines for partial tiles.

Levels are used to check walls for plumb and horizontal surfaces for level before tile is laid. Levels are also used to mark layouts for wall tile installations.

Carpenter's squares are used to establish perpendicular lines for floor tile installations.

Chalk lines are snapped to mark the reference lines for layouts.

Tape measures are essential for measuring rooms and creating layouts. They're also used to make sure that reference lines are perpendicular by using the 3-4-5 triangle method. (See page 41.)

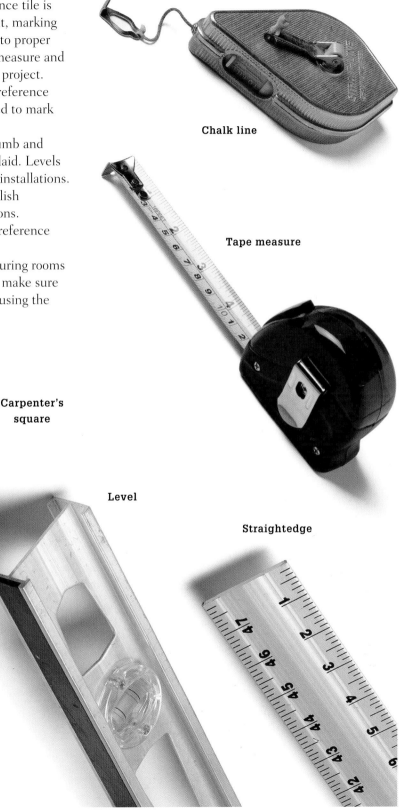

Chalk line

Tape measure

Carpenter's square

Level

Straightedge

Tools for Cutting Tile

Even though tile is a rigid material, it can be cut to fit a variety of applications. With the proper tools, tile can be trimmed, notched, and drilled. If you're planning only one tile project, consider renting the more expensive pieces of equipment.

Coping saws with rod saw blades are usually adequate for cutting soft tile, such as wall tile.

Tile nippers are used to create curves and circles. Tile is first marked with the scoring wheel of a hand-held tile cutter or a wet saw blade to create a cutting guide.

Hand-held tile cutters are used to snap tiles one at a time. They are often used for cutting mosaic tiles after they have been scored.

Tile stones file away rough edges left by tile nippers and hand-held tile cutters. Stones can also be used to shave off small amounts of tile for fitting.

Wet saws, also called "tile saws," employ water to cool both the blade and the tile during cutting. This tool is used primarily for cutting floor tile—especially natural stone tile—but it is also useful for quickly cutting large quantities of tile or notches in hard tile.

Diamond blades are used on hand-held wet saws and grinders to cut through the hardest tile materials such as pavers, marble, granite, slate, and other natural stone.

Tile cutters are quick, efficient tools for scoring and cutting straight lines in most types of light- to medium-weight tile.

Grinders come in handy for cutting granite and marble when equipped with a diamond blade. Cuts made with this hand tool will be less accurate than with a wet saw, so it is best used to cut tile for areas that will be covered with molding or fixtures.

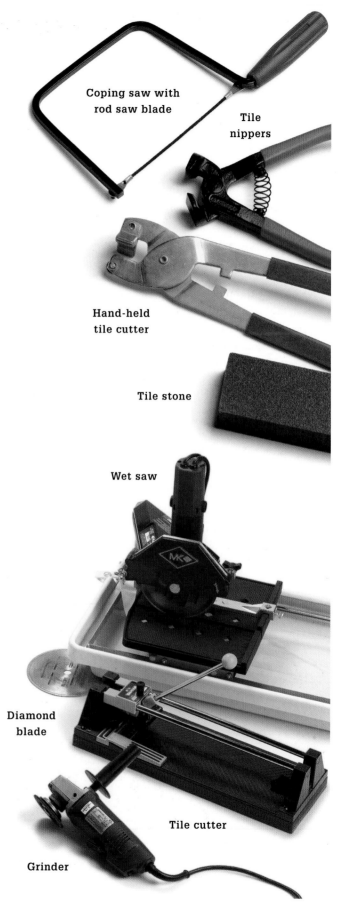

Coping saw with rod saw blade

Tile nippers

Hand-held tile cutter

Tile stone

Wet saw

Diamond blade

Tile cutter

Grinder

Tools for Setting & Grouting Tile

Laying tile requires quick, precise work, so it's wise to assemble the necessary supplies before you begin. You don't want to search for a tool with wet mortar already in place. Most of the tools required for setting and grouting tile are probably already in your tool box, so take an inventory before you head to the home center or hardware store.

Tile spacers are essential for achieving consistent spacing between tiles. They are set at corners of laid tile and are later removed so grout can be applied.

Grout sponges, buff rags, foam brushes, and grout sealer applicators are used after grout is applied. Grout sponges are used to wipe away grout residue, buff rags remove grout haze, and foam brushes and grout sealer applicators are for applying grout sealer.

Rubber mallets are used to gently tap tiles and set them evenly into mortar.

Needlenose pliers come in handy for removing spacers placed between tiles.

Caulk guns are used to fill expansion joints at the floor and base trim, at inside corners, and where tile meets surfaces made of other materials.

Grout floats are used to apply grout over tile and into joints. They are also used to remove excess grout from the surface of tiles after grout has been applied. For mosaic sheets, grout floats are handy for gently pressing tile into mortar.

Trowels are used to apply mortar to surfaces where tile will be laid and to apply mortar directly to the backs of cut tiles.

Buff rag

Grout sealer applicator

Grout sponge

Foam brush

Rubber mallet

Needlenose pliers

Tile spacers

Caulk gun

Trowel

Grout float

Notched trowel

Preparation Materials

The type of substrate you lay for ceramic tile will depend on where your new surface will be. Where moisture will be present, cementboard or fiber/cementboard should be installed. In other areas, plywood or cork can be suitable. Over concrete, isolation membrane may be required. Installing the proper foundation for your project will help prevent cracks and deterioration in laid tile.

Cork makes an excellent underlayment when sound control and warmth are an issue. In areas where moisture may be present, a waterproof membrane or sealant should be applied first.

Fiber/cementboard is a thin, high-density underlayment used in wet areas where floor height is a concern.

Cementboard remains stable even when exposed to moisture, so it is a good choice for wet tile areas, such as bathrooms.

Greenboard is drywall treated to withstand occasional moisture. It is a good choice for walls in bathrooms and other humid areas.

Plywood is a good, all-around underlayment in low-moisture areas. For ceramic tile installations, use ½" exterior-grade AC plywood.

Trowel-applied membrane is a paste form of water-proofing membrane that can be applied in areas that will be exposed to moisture.

Mesh tape or fiberglass tape is applied to cementboard seams, then a thin layer of mortar is applied over the tape to seal them.

Waterproofing membrane is applied over existing flooring and non-water-resistant substrate in areas that will be exposed to moisture.

Shower pan liners are used to create custom shower pans.

Isolation membrane is used either in strips or as a floor underlayment to cover cracks in concrete floors and protect tiles from movement.

Trowel-applied membrane

Waterproofing membrane

Fiberglass tape

Shower pan liner

Isolation membrane

Plywood

Cork

Fiber/ cementboard

Cementboard

Greenboard

Materials for Setting & Grouting Tile

To ensure your tiling project lasts, it's important to set and grout the tile properly. Follow directions for mixing and applying mortars, fortifiers, and adhesives. Then seal grout to keep your tile beautiful and long-lasting.

Thinset mortar is a cement-based adhesive that is purchased in dry form and prepared by adding liquid until a creamy consistency is achieved. Some mortars include a latex additive in the dry mix. Other mortars require a liquid latex additive.

Grout fills the spaces between tiles and is available in pre-tinted colors to match your tile. Grout width should be considered a decorative element of your tile project.

Latex fortifier is a liquid added to mortar to strengthen its bonding power. Some mortar powders include fortifier in the dry mix.

Grout sealer is applied with a sponge brush to ward off stains and make tile maintenance easier.

Wall tile mastic is used to install base-trim tile.

Wall and floor tile adhesive is available in pre-mixed formulas. Thinset mortar is, however, recommended for most flooring installations.

Thinset mortar

Grout

Wall tile mastic

Latex fortifier

Grout sealer

Floor tile adhesive

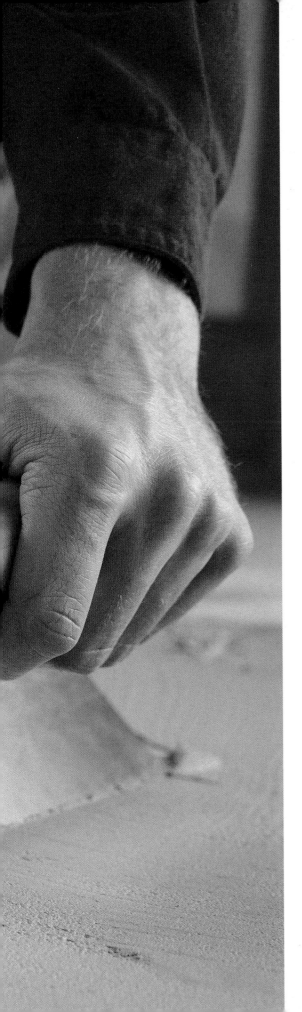

Appendix: Preparation Techniques

Like construction projects of all sorts, successful tile projects start with good preparation. Smooth, sound walls and well-supported, structurally sound floors are essential to long lasting, attractive tile installations. This chapter helps you evaluate existing wall and floor surfaces, then remove, replace, or repair them as necessary. It also leads you through the installation of a luxurious addition to any tile floor: a floor warming system. Floor warming systems are especially appealing in bathrooms and in rooms that tend to be cold in the winter, and as this project demonstrates, installing one is much easier than you might imagine.

In This Chapter:

- Evaluating & Preparing Floors
- Removing Floor Coverings
- Removing Underlayment
- Repairing Subfloors
- Installing Underlayment
- Installing a Floor-warming System
- Evaluating & Preparing Walls
- Removing Wall Surfaces
- Installing & Finishing Wallboard
- Installing Cementboard
- Installing Wall Membranes

Evaluating & Preparing Floors

The most important step in the success of your tile flooring project is evaluating and preparing the area. A well-done tile installation can last a lifetime—poor preparation can lead to a lifetime of cracked grout and broken tile headaches.

Because of the weight of ceramic and stone tile, it is important to assess the condition and placement of the joists, subfloor, and underlayment. Most tile installation cannot be done over existing flooring without the addition of underlayment. Check with your tile dealer for the specific requirements of the tile or stone you have chosen.

Though it may initially seem like more work, it is important to remove bathroom fixtures and vanities and non-plumbed kitchen islands for your floor tile project. Not only will this eliminate a great deal of cutting and fitting, it will allow you more flexibility in future remodeling choices.

Start by removing any fixtures or appliances in the work area, then baseboards, then the old flooring. Shovel old flooring debris through a window and into a wheelbarrow to speed up removal work. Cover doorways with sheet plastic to contain debris and dust during the removal process. Keep the dust and dirt from blowing throughout your house by covering air and heat vents with sheet plastic and masking tape.

How to Evaluate & Prepare Floors

Determining the number and type of coverings already on your floor is an important first step in evaluating its condition. Ceramic and stone tile floors have specific requirements that must be met to prevent surface cracks.

Measure vertical spaces in kitchens and bathrooms to ensure the proper fit of appliances and fixtures after the installation of tile. Use a sample of the tile and any additional underlayment as spacers while measuring.

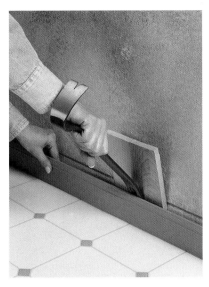

To remove baseboards, place a scrap board against the wall to avoid damaging the drywall. Remove the baseboard using a pry bar placed against the scrap board. Pry the baseboard at all nail locations. Number the baseboards as they are removed.

To prepare door jambs, measure the height of your underlayment and tile and mark the casing. Using a jamb saw, cut the casing at the mark.

To test the height of the door jamb, slide a piece of flooring under the door jamb to make sure it fits easily.

Anatomy of Your Floor ▸

A typical wood-frame floor consists of several layers that work together to provide the required structural support and desired appearance. At the bottom of the floor are the joists, the 2 × 10 or larger framing members that support the weight of the floor. Joists are typically spaced 16" apart on-center. The subfloor is nailed to the joists. Most subfloors installed in the 1970s or later are made of ¾" tongue-and-groove plywood, but in older homes, the subfloor often consists of 1"-thick wood planks nailed diagonally across the floor joists. On top of the subfloor, most builders place a ½" plywood underlayment. For many types of floor coverings, adhesive or mortar is spread on the underlayment prior to installing the floor cover.

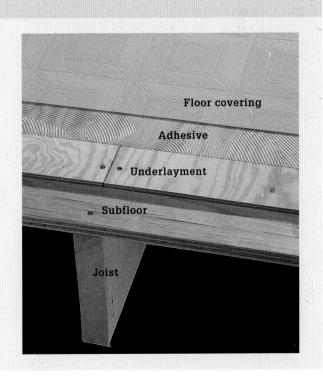

Floor covering

Adhesive

Underlayment

Subfloor

Joist

How to Remove a Toilet

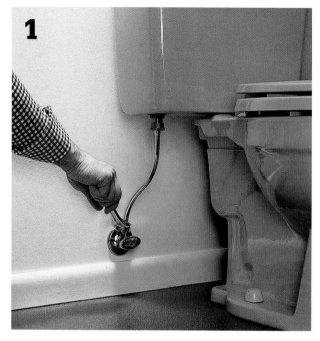

1

Turn off the water at the shutoff valve and flush the toilet to empty the tank. Use a sponge to soak up remaining water in the tank and bowl. Disconnect the supply tube, using an adjustable wrench.

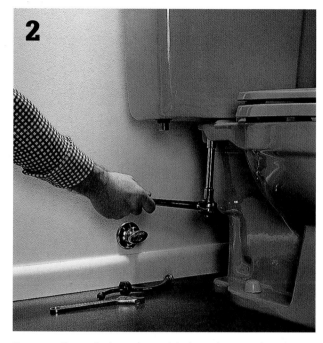

2

Remove the nuts from the tank bolts, using a ratchet wrench. Carefully remove the tank and set it aside.

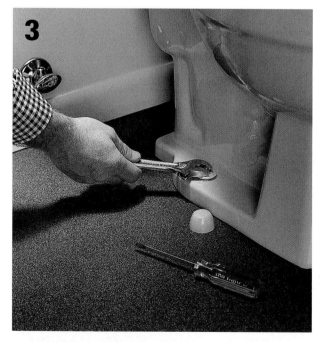

3

Pry off the floor bolt trim caps, then remove the nuts from the floor bolts. Rock the bowl from side to side to break the seal, then lift the toilet from the bolts and set it aside. Wear rubber gloves while cleaning up any water that spills from the toilet trap.

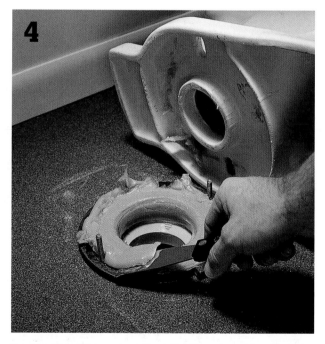

4

Scrape the old wax from the toilet flange, and plug the drain opening with a damp rag so sewer gas doesn't escape into the house. If you're going to reinstall the old toilet, clean the old wax and plumber's putty from around the horn and base of the toilet.

How to Remove Sinks

Self-rimming sink: Disconnect the plumbing, then slice through any caulk or sealant between the sink rim and the countertop, using a utility knife. Lift the sink off the countertop.

Pedestal sink: Disconnect the plumbing. If the sink and pedestal are bolted together, disconnect them. Remove the pedestal first, supporting the sink from below with 2 × 4s. Slice through any caulk or sealant. (Inset) Lift the sink off the wall brackets.

How to Remove Vanities

Detach any mounting hardware, located underneath the countertop inside the vanity.

Slice through any caulk or sealant between the wall and the countertop. Remove the countertop from the vanity, using a pry bar if necessary.

Remove the screws or nails (usually driven through the back rail of the cabinet) that anchor the vanity to the wall.

Removing Floor Coverings

When removing old floor coverings, thorough and careful removal work is essential to the quality of a new floor tile or stone installation.

The difficulty of flooring removal depends on the type of floor covering and the method that was used to install it. Carpet and perimeter-bond vinyl are generally quite easy to remove, and vinyl tiles are relatively simple. Full-spread sheet vinyl can be difficult to remove, however, and removing ceramic tile is a lot of work.

With any removal project, be sure to keep your tool blades sharp and avoid damaging the underlayment if you plan to reuse it. If you'll be replacing the underlayment, it may be easier to remove the old underlayment along with the floor covering (see pages 222 through 227).

Resilient flooring from before 1986 might contain asbestos, so consult an asbestos containment expert or have a sample tested before beginning removal. Even if no asbestos is present, wear a good quality dust mask.

Tools & Materials ▸

Floor scraper	Hand maul
Utility knife	Masonry chisel
Spray bottle	Flat pry bar
Wallboard knife	End-cutting nippers
Wet/dry vacuum	Liquid dishwashing
Heat gun	detergent
Dust mask	Broom

Use a floor scraper to remove resilient flooring products and to scrape off leftover adhesives or backings. The long handle provides leverage and force, and it allows you to work in a comfortable standing position. A scraper will remove most flooring, but you may need to use other tools to finish the job.

How to Remove Sheet Vinyl

1

Remove base moldings, if necessary. Use a utility knife to cut old flooring into strips about a foot wide.

2

Pull up as much flooring as possible by hand, gripping the strips close to the floor to minimize tearing.

3

Cut stubborn sheet vinyl into strips about 5" wide. Starting at a wall, peel up as much of the floor covering as possible. If the felt backing remains, spray a solution of water and liquid dishwashing detergent under the surface layer to help separate the backing. Use a wallboard knife to scrape up particularly stubborn patches.

4

Scrape up the remaining sheet vinyl and backing, using a floor scraper. If necessary, spray the backing again with the soap solution to loosen it. Sweep up the debris, then finish the cleanup with a wet/dry vacuum. *Tip: Fill the vacuum with about an inch of water to help contain dust.*

How to Remove Vinyl Tile

Remove base moldings, if necessary. Starting at a loose seam, use a long-handled floor scraper to remove tiles. To remove stubborn tiles, soften the adhesive with a heat gun, then use a wallboard knife to pry up the tile and scrape off the underlying adhesive.

Remove stubborn adhesive or backing by wetting the floor with a water/detergent mixture, then scraping with a floor scraper.

How to Remove Ceramic Tile

Remove base moldings, if necessary. Knock out tile using a hand maul and masonry chisel. If possible, start in a space between tiles where the grout has loosened. Be careful when working around fragile fixtures, such as drain flanges.

If you plan to reuse the underlayment, use a floor scraper to remove any remaining adhesive. You may have to use a belt sander with a coarse sanding belt to grind off stubborn adhesive.

How to Remove Carpet

Using a utility knife, cut around metal threshold strips to free the carpet. Remove the threshold strips with a flat pry bar.

Cut the carpet into pieces small enough to be easily removed. Roll up the carpet and remove it from the room, then remove the padding. *Note: Padding often is stapled to the floor, and usually will come up in pieces as you roll it up.*

Using end-cutting nippers or pliers, remove all staples from the floor. *Tip: If you plan to lay new carpet, do not remove the tackless strips unless they are damaged.*

Variation: To remove glued-down carpet, first cut it into strips with a utility knife, then pull up as much material as you can. Scrape up the remaining cushion material and adhesive with a floor scraper.

Removing Underlayment

Flooring contractors routinely remove the underlayment along with the floor covering before installing new flooring. This saves time and makes it possible to install new underlayment that is ideally suited to ceramic and stone tile. Do-it-yourselfers using this technique should make sure they cut flooring into pieces that can be easily handled.

Tools & Materials ▸

Goggles
Gloves
Circular saw with
    carbide-tipped blade
Flat pry bar
Reciprocating saw
Wood chisel
Screwdriver
Hammer

Warning ▸

This floor removal method releases flooring particles into the air. Be sure the flooring you are removing does not contain asbestos.

Tip ▸

Examine fasteners to see how the underlayment is attached. Use a screwdriver to expose the heads of the fasteners. If the underlayment has been screwed down, you will need to remove the floor covering and then unscrew the underlayment.

Remove underlayment and floor covering as though they were a single layer. This is an effective removal strategy with any floor covering that is bonded to the underlayment.

How to Remove Underlayment

1

Remove base moldings, if necessary. Adjust the cutting depth of a circular saw to equal the combined thickness of your floor covering and underlayment. Using a carbide-tipped blade, cut the floor covering and underlayment into squares measuring about 3 ft. square. Be sure to wear safety goggles and gloves.

2

Use a reciprocating saw to extend cuts close to the edges of walls. Hold the blade at a slight angle to the floor, and try not to damage walls or cabinets. Do not cut deeper than the underlayment. Use a wood chisel to complete cuts near cabinets.

3

Separate the underlayment from the subfloor, using a flat pry bar and hammer. Remove and discard the sections of underlayment and floor covering immediately, watching for exposed nails.

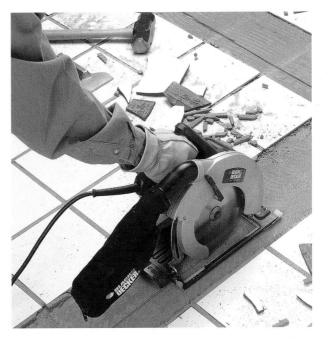

Variation: If your existing floor is ceramic tile over plywood underlayment, use a hand maul and masonry chisel to chip away the tile along the cutting lines before making the cuts.

Repairing Subfloors

A solid, securely fastened subfloor minimizes floor movement and prevents grout and tile cracking.

After removing the old underlayment, inspect the subfloor for loose seams, moisture damage, cracks, and other flaws. Bulges and dips may require repairs to the joists, or simply application of a leveler.

Concrete floors also need to be evaluated for cracks and holes, which can be repaired, and dips and bulges, which can be filled with concrete leveler. Concrete floors may also require an isolation membrane (see page 235) to further protect tiles from cracking.

Tools & Materials ▸

Trowel	2" deck screws
Straightedge	3" lag screws
Framing square	Floor leveler/
Drill	floor scraper
Circular saw	Plywood
Cat's paw	2 × 4 lumber
Wood chisel	10d common nails
Ratchet wrench	16d common nails
Vacuum	Long-nap paint roller
Gage rake	Reciprocating saw
Hammer	Masonry chisel
Tape measure	

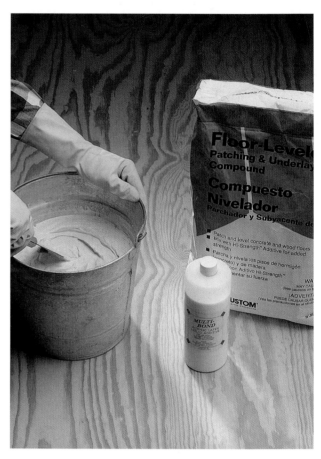

Floor leveler is used to fill in dips and low spots in plywood subfloors. Mix the leveler according to the manufacturer's directions, adding a latex or acrylic additive.

Before installing new underlayment and floor covering, refasten any sections of loose subfloor to floor joists, using deck screws.

How to Apply Floor Leveler on Subfloor

Mix the leveler according to the manufacturer's directions, then spread it onto the subfloor with a trowel. Build up the leveler in thin layers to avoid overfilling the area.

Check with a straightedge to make sure the filled area is even with the surrounding area; if necessary, apply more leveler. Allow the leveler to dry, then shave off any ridges with the edge of a trowel, or sand it smooth, if necessary.

How to Replace a Section of Subfloor

Cut out damaged areas of the subfloor. Use a framing square to mark a rectangle around the damage—make sure two sides of the rectangle are centered over floor joists. Remove nails along the lines, using a cat's paw. Make the cut using a circular saw adjusted so the blade cuts through only the subfloor. Use a chisel to complete the cuts near walls.

Remove the damaged section, then nail two 2 × 4 blocks between the joists, centered under the cut edges for added support. If possible, endnail the blocks from below; otherwise toenail them from above, using 10d nails.

Measure the cutout section, then cut a patch to fit, using material of the same thickness as the original subfloor. Fasten the patch to the joists and blocks, using 2" deck screws spaced about 5" apart.

How to Reinforce Floor Joists

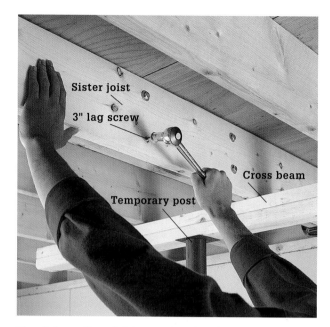

To reinforce floor joists, attach a sister joist alongside the existing joist, using 3" lag screws. The sister joist should run the full length of the original floor joist. Sister joists should be installed wherever existing joists are damaged, and may be required under floor areas that will support the additional weight of bathtubs or whirlpools.

Install a support post and cross beam below a sagging floor. Adjust the post to rough height, then position the post so it is plumb. Raise the post by turning the threaded base plate; pressure will hold the post and beam in place. Raise no more than ¼" per week, until floor above is level. Building codes may restrict the use of adjustable posts, so consult an inspector.

How to Reduce a Bulging Joist

Check the area with a level to find the highest point. Move the level to different points, noting the gap between the floor and the ends of the level. Mark the highest point of the bulge, and measure from an element that extends below the floor, such as an exterior wall or a heating duct. Use this measurement to mark the high point on the bulging joist from below the floor.

From the bottom edge, make a straight cut into the problem joist below the high point mark, using a reciprocating saw. Make the cut ¾ the depth of the joist. Allow several weeks for the joist to relax and straighten, checking the floor periodically with a level. Don't load the floor above the joist with excessive weight.

When the joist has settled, reinforce it by nailing a board of the same size to the joist. Make the reinforcement piece at least 6 ft. long, and drive 16d common nails in staggered pairs, 12" apart. Drive a row of three nails on either side of the cut in the joist.

How to Patch Concrete Floors

Clean the floor with a vacuum, and remove any loose or flaking concrete with a masonry chisel and hammer. Mix a batch of vinyl floor patching compound, following manufacturer's directions. Apply the compound using a smooth trowel, slightly overfilling the cavity. Smooth the patch flush with the surface.

After the compound has cured fully, use a floor scraper to scrape the patched areas smooth.

How to Apply Floor Leveler on Concrete

Remove any loose material and clean the concrete thoroughly; the surface must be free of dust, dirt, oils, and paint. Apply an even layer of concrete primer to the entire surface, using a long-nap paint roller. Let the primer dry completely.

Following the manufacturer's instructions, mix the floor leveler with water. The batch should be large enough to cover the entire floor area to the desired thickness (up to 1"). Pour the leveler over the floor.

Distribute the leveler evenly, using a gage rake or spreader. Work quickly: The leveler begins to harden in 15 minutes. Use a trowel to feather the edges and create a smooth transition with an uncovered area. Let the leveler dry for 24 hours.

Installing Underlayment

Ceramic and natural stone tile floors often require an underlayment that stands up to moisture, such as cementboard. If you will use your old flooring as underlayment, apply an embossing leveler to prepare it for the new installation (see below, right).

When installing new underlayment, make sure it is securely attached to the subfloor in all areas, including below all movable appliances. Notch the underlayment to fit room contours. Around door casings and other moldings, undercut the moldings and insert the underlayment beneath them.

Plywood is typically used as an underlayment for vinyl flooring and for ceramic tile installations in dry areas. For ceramic tile, use ½" exterior-grade AC plywood. Do not use particleboard, oriented-strand board, or treated lumber as underlayment for tile.

Fiber/cementboard is a thin, high-density underlayment used under ceramic tile in situations where floor height is a concern. (For installation, follow the steps for cementboard, on page 246.)

Cementboard is used exclusively for ceramic or stone tile installations. It remains stable even when exposed to moisture and is therefore the best underlayment to use in areas likely to get wet, such as bathrooms.

Isolation membrane is used to protect ceramic tile installations from movement that may occur on cracked concrete floors. It is often used to cover individual cracks, but it can also be used over an entire floor. Isolation membrane is also available in a liquid form that can be poured over the project area.

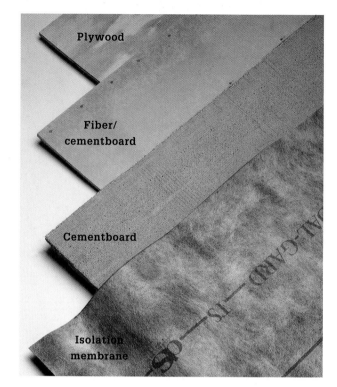

Plywood

Fiber/ cementboard

Cementboard

Isolation membrane

Tip ▸

Embossing leveler is a mortar-like substance used for preparing well-adhered resilient flooring or ceramic tile for use as an underlayment. Mix the leveler according to the manufacturer's directions, and spread it thinly over the floor with a flat-edged trowel. Wipe away any excess, making sure all dips and indentations are filled. Work quickly—embossing leveler begins to set in 10 minutes. After the leveler dries, scrape away ridges and high spots with the trowel.

Tools & Materials ▸

Drill	Plywood underlayment
Circular saw	1" deck screws
Wallboard knife	Floor-patching
Power sander	compound
¼" notched trowel	Latex additive
Straightedge	Thinset mortar
Utility knife	1½" galvanized deck
Jigsaw with carbide	screws
blade	Cementboard
⅛" notched trowel	Fiberglass-mesh
Flooring roller	wallboard tape

How to Install Plywood Underlayment

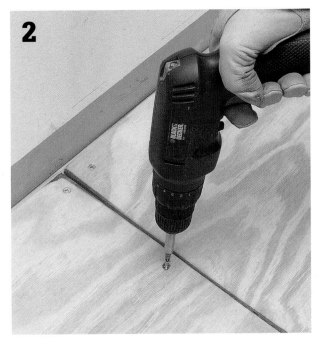

Begin by installing a full sheet of plywood along the longest wall, making sure the underlayment seams will not be aligned with the subfloor seams. Fasten the plywood to the subfloor, using 1" deck screws driven every 6" along the edges and at 8" intervals in the field of the sheet.

Continue fastening sheets of plywood to the subfloor, driving the screw heads slightly below the underlayment surface. Leave ¼" expansion gaps at the walls and between sheets. Offset seams in subsequent rows.

Using a circular saw or jigsaw, notch plywood to meet existing flooring in doorways, then fasten the notched sheets to the subfloor.

Mix floor-patching compound and latex or acrylic additive, according to the manufacturer's directions. Spread it over seams and screw heads with a wallboard knife.

Let the patching compound dry, then sand the patched areas, using a power sander.

How to Install Cementboard

Mix thinset mortar (see page 260) according to the manufacturer's directions. Starting at the longest wall, spread the mortar on the subfloor in a figure-eight pattern, using a ¼" notched trowel. Spread only enough mortar for one sheet at a time. Set the cementboard on the mortar with the rough side up, making sure the edges are offset from the subfloor seams.

Fasten the cementboard to the subfloor, using 1½" galvanized deck screws driven every 6" along edges and 8" throughout the sheet. Drive the screw heads flush with the surface. Continue spreading mortar and installing sheets along the wall.

Cut cementboard pieces as necessary, leaving a ⅛" gap at all joints and a ¼" gap along the room perimeter. For straight cuts, use a utility knife to score a line through the fiber-mesh layer just beneath the surface, then snap the board along the scored line.

To cut holes, notches, or irregular shapes, use a jigsaw with a carbide blade. Continue installing cementboard sheets to cover the entire floor. Inset: A flange extender or additional wax ring may be needed to ensure a proper toilet installation after additional layers of underlayment have been installed in a bathroom.

Place fiberglass-mesh wallboard tape over the seams. Use a wallboard knife to apply thinset mortar to the seams, filling the gaps between sheets and spreading a thin layer of mortar over the tape. Allow the mortar to cure for two days before starting the tile installation.

How to Install Isolation Membrane

Thoroughly clean the subfloor, then apply thinset mortar (see page 260) with a ⅛" notched trowel. Start spreading the mortar along a wall in a section as wide as the membrane and 8 to 10 ft. long. *Note: For some membranes, you must use a bonding material other than mortar. Read and follow label directions.*

Roll out the membrane over the mortar. Cut the membrane to fit tightly against the walls, using a straightedge and utility knife.

Starting in the center of the membrane, use a heavy flooring roller (available at rental centers) to smooth out the surface toward the edges. This frees trapped air and presses out excess bonding material.

Repeat steps 1 through 3, cutting the membrane as necessary at the walls and obstacles, until the floor is completely covered with membrane. Do not overlap the seams, but make sure they are tight. Allow the mortar to cure for two days before installing the tile.

Installing a Floor-warming System

Floor-warming systems require very little energy to run and are designed to heat ceramic tile floors only; they generally are not used as sole heat sources for rooms.

A typical floor-warming system consists of one or more thin mats containing electric resistance wires that heat up when energized, like an electric blanket. The mats are installed beneath the tile and are hardwired to a 120-volt GFCI circuit. A thermostat controls the temperature, and a timer turns the system on or off automatically.

The system shown in this project includes two plastic mesh mats, each with its own power lead that is wired directly to the thermostat. The mats are laid over a concrete floor and then covered with thinset adhesive and ceramic tile. If you have a wood subfloor, install cementboard before laying the mats.

A crucial part of installing this system is to perform several resistance checks to make sure the heating wires have not been damaged during shipping or during the installation.

Electrical service required for a floor-warming system is based on size. A smaller system may connect to an existing GFCI circuit, but a larger one will need a dedicated circuit; follow the manufacturer's requirements.

To order a floor-warming system, contact the manufacturer or dealer. In most cases, you can send them plans and they'll custom-fit a system for your project area.

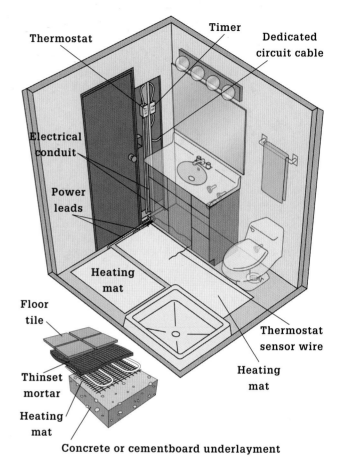

Thermostat · Timer · Dedicated circuit cable · Electrical conduit · Power leads · Heating mat · Floor tile · Thinset mortar · Heating mat · Thermostat sensor wire · Heating mat · Concrete or cementboard underlayment

Tools & Materials ▶

Multi-tester
Drill
Plumb bob
Chisel
Tubing cutter
Combination tool
Vacuum
Chalk line
Grinder
Hot-glue gun
Fish tape
Tile tools (page 41)
Floor-warming system
Hammer

2½" × 4" double-gang electrical box
Single-gang electrical box
½"-dia. thin-wall conduit
Setscrew fittings
12-gauge NM cable
Cable clamps
Double-sided tape
Electrical tape
Insulated cable clamps
Wire connectors
Tile materials
Tape Measure

Tip ▶

Floor-warming systems must be installed on a circuit with adequate amperage and a GFCI breaker (some systems have built-in GFCIs). Smaller systems may tie into an existing circuit, but larger ones need a dedicated circuit. Follow local building and electrical codes that apply to your project.

How to Install a Floor-warming System

Check the resistance value (ohms) of each heating mat, using a digital multi-tester. Record the reading. Compare your reading to the factory-tested reading noted by the manufacturer—your reading must fall within the acceptable range determined by the manufacturer. If it does not, the mat has been damaged and should not be installed; contact the manufacturer for assistance.

Install electrical boxes for the thermostat and timer at an accessible location. Remove the wall surface to expose the framing, then locate the boxes approximately 60" from the floor, making sure the power leads of the heating mats will reach the double-gang electrical box. Mount a 2½"-deep × 4"-wide double-gang electrical box (for the thermostat) to the stud closest to the determined location, and a single-gang electrical box (for the timer) on the other side of the stud.

Use a plumb bob to mark points on the bottom plate directly below the two knockouts on the thermostat box. At each mark, drill a ½" hole through the top of the plate, then drill two more holes as close as possible to the floor through the side of the plate, intersecting the top holes. (The holes will be used to route the power leads and thermostat sensor wire.) Clean up the holes with a chisel to ensure smooth routing.

Setscrew
fittings

Cut two lengths of ½" thin-wall electrical conduit to fit between the thermostat box and the bottom plate, using a tubing cutter. Place the bottom end of each length of conduit about ¼" into the holes in the bottom plate, and fasten the top end to the thermostat box, using a setscrew fitting. *Note: If you are installing three or more mats, use ¾" conduit instead of ½".*

(continued)

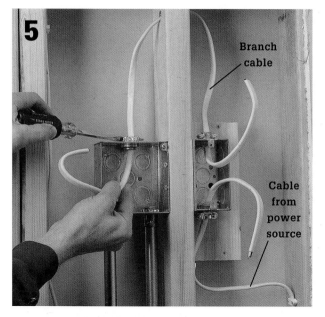

5

Run 12-gauge NM electrical cable from the service panel (power source) to the timer box. Attach the cable to the box with a cable clamp, leaving 8" of extra cable extending from the box. Drill a ⅝" hole through the center of the stud, about 12" above the boxes. Run a short branch cable from the timer box to the thermostat box, securing both ends with clamps. The branch cable should make a smooth curve where it passes through the stud.

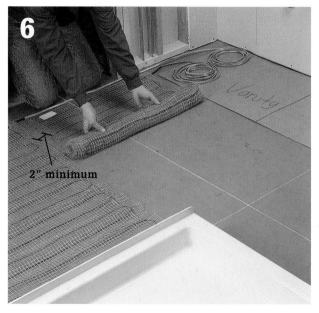

6

Branch cable

Cable from power source

2" minimum

Vacuum the floor thoroughly. Plan the ceramic tile layout and snap reference lines for the tile installation (pages 38 to 44). Spread the heating mats onto the floor with the power leads closest to the electrical boxes. Position the mats 3" to 6" away from walls, showers, bathtubs, and toilet flanges. You can lay the mats into the kick space of a vanity, but not under the vanity cabinet or over expansion joints in a concrete slab. Set the edges of the mats close together, but do not overlap them. The heating wires in one mat must be at least 2" from the wires in the neighboring mat.

7

Confirm that the power leads still reach the thermostat box. Secure the mats to the floor, using strips of double-sided tape spaced every 24". Make sure the mats are lying flat with no wrinkles or ripples. Press down firmly to secure the mats to the tape.

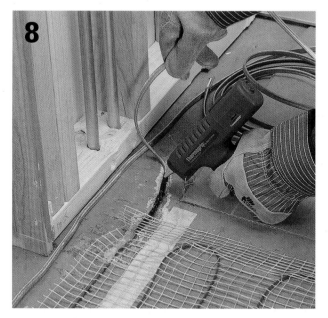

8

Create recesses in the floor for the connections between the power leads and the heating-mat wires, using a grinder or a cold chisel and hammer. These insulated connections are too thick to lay under the tile and must be recessed to within ⅛" of the floor. Clean away any debris, and secure the connections in the recesses with a bead of hot glue.

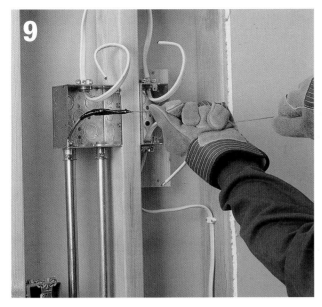

Thread a steel fish tape down one of the conduits, and attach the ends of the power leads to the fish tape, using electrical tape. Pull the fish tape and leads up through the conduit. Disconnect the fish tape, and secure the leads to the box with insulated cable clamps. Cut off the excess from the leads, leaving 8" extending from the clamps.

Feed the heat sensor wire down through the remaining conduit and weave it into the mesh of the nearest mat. Use dabs of hot glue to secure the sensor wire directly between two blue resistance wires, extending it 6" to 12" into the mat. Test the resistance of the heating mats with a multi-tester (step 1, page 237) to make sure the resistance wires have not been damaged. Record the reading.

Install the ceramic floor tile (pages 56 to 63). Use thinset mortar as an adhesive, and spread it carefully over the floor and mats with a ⅜" × ¼" square-notched trowel. Check the resistance of the mats periodically during the tile installation. If a mat becomes damaged, clean up any exposed mortar and contact the manufacturer. When the installation is complete, check the resistance of the mats once again and record the reading.

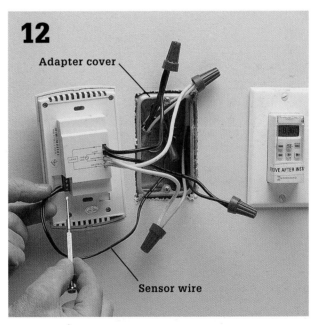

Adapter cover

Sensor wire

Install an adapter cover to the thermostat box, then patch the wall opening with drywall. Complete the wiring connections for the thermostat and timer, following the manufacturer's instructions. Attach the sensor wire to the thermostat setscrew connection. Apply the manufacturer's wiring labels to the thermostat box and service panel. Mount the thermostat and timer. Complete the circuit connection at the service panel or branch connection. After the flooring materials have fully cured, test the system.

Evaluating & Preparing Walls

The substrate for wall tiles must be stable; that is, it must not expand and contract in response to changes in temperature or humidity. For this reason, you need to strip all wallpaper before tiling, even if the paper has been painted. Similarly, remove any type of wood paneling before tiling a wall. Even painted walls need some preparation. For example, paint that's likely to peel needs to be sanded thoroughly before the project starts.

Smooth, concrete walls can be tiled, but the concrete has to be prepared. Scrub it with a concrete cleaner, then apply a concrete bonding agent. Use a grinder to smooth any unevenness. Install an isolation membrane (see page 235) to keep the tile from cracking if the walls crack, which is common.

Brick or block walls are a good substrate for tiling, but the surface is not smooth enough to be tiled without additional preparation. Mix extra portland cement into brick mortar and apply a smooth, even skim coat to the walls and let it dry thoroughly before beginning the tile project.

Existing tile can be tiled over as long as the glaze has been roughened enough for the adhesive to adhere properly. Remember, though, that the new tile will protrude quite a way from the wall. You'll need to accommodate for this on the edges and around receptacles, switches, windows or doors, and other obstacles.

In some cases, you'll find that it's easiest to remove the old substrate and install new (see pages 242 to 243). Even if you're working with an appropriate substrate in good condition, you will need to evaluate the wall to make sure it is plumb and flat, and fix surface flaws before you begin your wall tiling project.

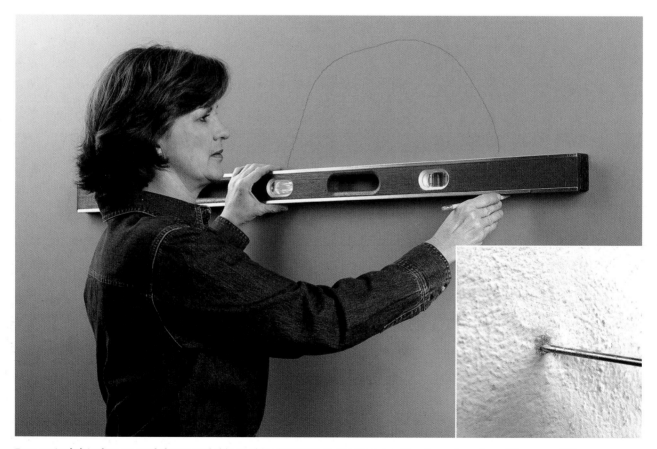

Run a straightedge up and down and side-to-side along wall surfaces and outline the valleys. Any difference of ¼" or more must be filled with joint compound using a 12" taping knife. You may need to apply a number of thin layers for best results. (Inset) Some plaster surfaces are softer than others. This high lime content plaster is too soft to serve as a backing surface for tile.

How to Patch Holes

Patching small holes: Fill smooth holes with spackle, then sand, then smooth. Cover ragged holes with a repair patch, then apply two coats of spackle or wallboard compound. Use a damp sponge or wet sander to smooth the repair area, then sand when dry, if necessary.

Patching large holes: Draw cutting lines around the hole, then cut away the damaged area, using a wallboard saw. Place plywood strips behind the opening and drive wallboard screws to hold them in place. Drive screws through the patch and into the backers. Cover the joints with wallboard tape and finish with compound.

Checking & Correcting Out-of-Plumb Walls

1

Use a plumb bob to determine if corners are plumb. A wall more than ½" out of plumb should be corrected before tiling.

2

If the wall is out of plumb, use a long level to mark a plumb line the entire height of the wall. Remove the wall covering from the out-of-plumb wall.

3

Cut and install shims on all the studs to create a new, plumb surface for attaching backing materials. Draw arrows at the shim highpoints to mark for drywall screw placement.

Removing Wall Surfaces

You may have to remove and replace interior wall surfaces before starting your tiling project. Most often, the material you'll be removing is wallboard, but you may be removing plaster or ceramic tile. Removing wall surfaces is a messy job, but it is not difficult. Before you begin, shut off the power and inspect the wall for wiring and plumbing.

Make sure you wear appropriate safety gear—glasses and dust masks—since you will be generating dust and small pieces of debris. Use plastic sheeting to close off doorways and air vents to prevent dust from spreading throughout the house. Protect floor surfaces and the bathtub with rosin paper securely taped down. Dust and debris will find their way under drop cloths and will quickly scratch your floor or tub surfaces.

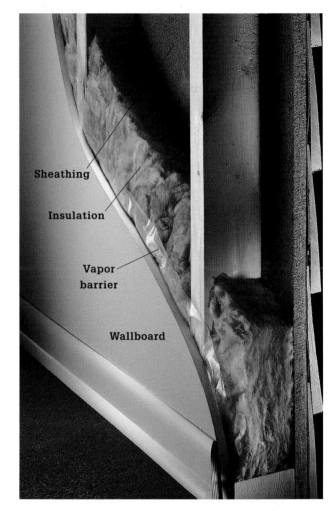

Sheathing

Insulation

Vapor barrier

Wallboard

Tools & Materials ▸

Utility knife	Reciprocating saw
Pry bar	with bimetal blade
Circular saw with	Heavy tarp
demolition blade	Hammer
Straightedge	Protective eyewear
Maul	Dust mask
Masonry chisel	Rosin paper
	2 × 4

How to Remove Wallboard

Remove baseboards and other trim, and prepare the work area. Make a ½"-deep cut from floor to ceiling, using a circular saw. Use a utility knife to finish the cuts at the top and bottom and to cut through the taped horizontal seam where the wall meets the ceiling surface.

Insert the end of a pry bar into the cut near one corner of the opening. Pull the pry bar until the wallboard breaks, then tear away the broken pieces. Take care to avoid damaging the wallboard outside the project area.

How to Remove Plaster

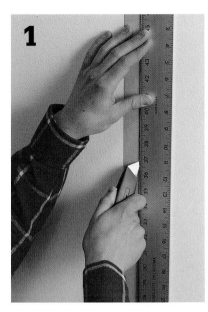

Remove baseboards and other trim and prepare the work area. Score the cutting line several times with a utility knife, using a straightedge as a guide. The line should be at least ⅛" deep.

Break the plaster along the edge by holding a scrap piece of 2 × 4 on edge just inside the scored line, and rapping it with a hammer. Use a pry bar to remove the remaining plaster.

Cut through the lath along the edges of the plaster, using a reciprocating saw or jigsaw. Remove the lath from the studs, using a pry bar.

How to Remove Ceramic Wall Tile

Be sure the floor is covered with a heavy tarp, and the electricity and water are shut off. Knock a small starter hole into the bottom of the wall, using a maul and masonry chisel.

Begin cutting out small sections of the wall by inserting a reciprocating saw with a bimetal blade into the hole, and cutting along grout lines. Be careful when sawing near pipes and wiring.

Cut the entire wall surface into small sections, removing each section as it is cut. Be careful not to cut through studs.

Installing & Finishing Wallboard

Regular wallboard is an appropriate backer for ceramic tile in dry locations. Greenboard, a moisture-resistent form of wallboard, is good for kitchens and the dry areas of bathrooms. Tub and shower surrounds and kitchen backsplashes should have a cementboard backer.

Wallboard panels are available in 4 × 8-ft. or 4 × 10-ft. sheets, and in ⅜", ½", and ⅝" thicknesses. For new walls, ½" thick is standard.

Install wallboard panels so that seams fall over the center of framing members, not at sides. Use all-purpose wallboard compound and paper joint tape to finish seams.

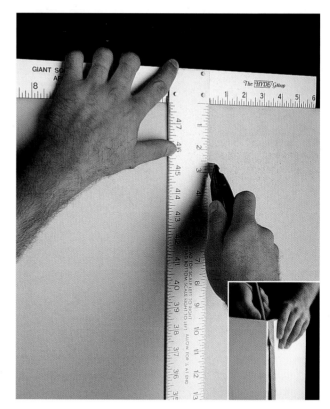

Score wallboard face paper with a utility knife, using a drywall T-square as a guide. Bend the panel away from the scored line until the core breaks, then cut through the back paper (inset) with a utility knife, and separate the pieces.

Tools & Materials ▸

Tape measure	Screw gun
Utility knife	Wallboard
Wallboard	Wallboard tape
T-square	1¼" coarse-thread
6" and 12"	wallboard screws
wallboard knives	Wallboard compound
150-grit sanding	Metal inside corner bead
sponge	Taping knife

How to Install and Finish Wallboard

1

Install panels with their tapered edges butted together. Fasten with 1¼" wallboard screws, driven every 8" along the edges, and every 12" in the field. Drive screws deep enough to dimple surface without ripping face paper (inset).

2

Finish the seams by applying an even bed layer of wallboard compound over the seam, about ⅛" thick, using a 6" taping knife.

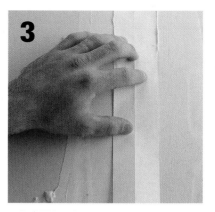

3

Center the wallboard tape over the seam and lightly embed it into the compound, making sure it's smooth and straight.

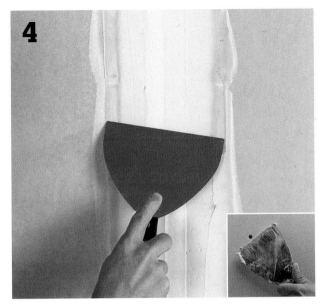

4

Smooth the tape with the taping knife. Apply enough pressure to force compound from underneath the tape, leaving the tape flat and with a thin layer underneath. Cover all exposed screw heads with the first of three coats of compound (inset). Let compound dry overnight.

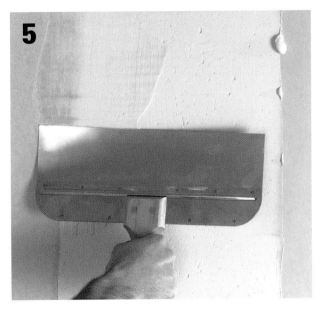

5

Second-coat the seams with a thin, even layer of compound, using a 12" knife. Feather the sides of the compound first, holding the blade almost flat and applying pressure to the outside of the blade so the blade just skims over the center of the seam.

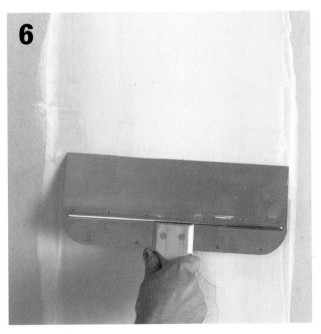

6

After feathering both sides, make a pass down the center of the seam, leaving the seam smooth and even, the edges feathered out even with the wallboard surface. Completely cover the joint tape. Let the second coat dry, then apply a third coat, using the 12" knife. After the third coat dries completely, sand the compound lightly with a wallboard sander or a 150-grit sanding sponge.

Tip ▸

Finish any inside corners, using paper-faced metal inside corner bead to produce straight, durable corners with little fuss. Embed the bead into a thin layer of compound, then smooth the paper with a taping knife. Apply two finish coats to the corner, then sand the compound smooth.

Installing Cementboard

Use tile backer board as the substrate for tile walls in wet areas. Unlike wallboard, tile backer won't break down and cause damage if water gets behind the tile. The three basic types of tile backer are cementboard, fiber-cement board, and Dens-Shield.

Though water cannot damage either cementboard or fiber-cement board, it can pass through them. To protect the framing members, install a water barrier of 4-mil plastic or 15# building paper behind the backer.

Dens-Shield has a waterproof acrylic facing that provides the water barrier. It cuts and installs much like wallboard, but it requires galvanized screws to prevent corrosion and must be sealed with caulk at all untaped joints and penetrations.

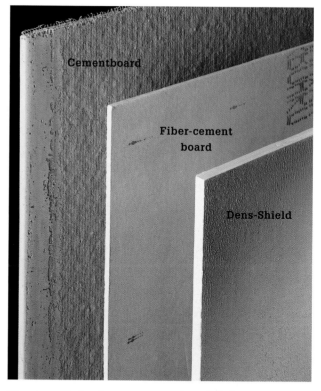

Common tile backers are cementboard, fiber-cementboard, and Dens-Shield. Cementboard is made from portland cement and sand reinforced by an outer layer of fiberglass mesh. Fiber-cement board is made similarly, but with a fiber reinforcement integrated throughout the panel. Dens-Shield is a water-resistant gypsum board with a waterproof acrylic facing.

Tools & Materials ▸

Utility knife	Stapler
T-square	Drill
Drill with a small masonry bit	4-mil plastic sheeting
	Cementboard
Hammer	1¼" cementboard screws
Jigsaw with a bimetal blade	Cementboard joint tape
	Latex-portland cement mortar
Wallboard knife	
Carbide-tipped cutter	15# building paper

How to Install Cementboard

Staple a water barrier of 4-mil plastic sheeting or 15# building paper over the framing. Overlap seams by several inches, and leave the sheets long at the perimeter. *Note: Framing for cementboard must be 16" on-center; steel studs must be 20-gauge.*

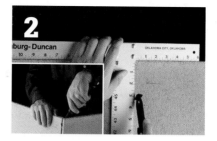

Cut cementboard by scoring through the mesh just below the surface, using a utility knife or carbide-tipped cutter. Snap the panel back, then cut through the back-side mesh (inset). *Note: For tile applications, the rough face of the board is the front.*

Make cutouts for pipes and other penetrations by drilling a series of holes through the board, using a small masonry bit. Tap the hole out with a hammer or a scrap of pipe. Cut holes along edges with a jigsaw and bimetal blade.

Install the sheets horizontally. Where possible, use full pieces to avoid cut-and-butted seams, which are difficult to fasten. If there are vertical seams, stagger them between rows. Leave a ⅛" gap between sheets at vertical seams and corners. Use spacers to set the bottom row of panels ¼" above the tub or shower base. Fasten the sheets with 1¼" cementboard screws, driven every 8" for walls and every 6" for ceilings. Drive the screws ½" from the edges to prevent crumbling. If the studs are steel, don't fasten within 1" of the top track.

Cover the joints and corners with cementboard joint tape (alkali-resistant fiberglass mesh) and latex-portland cement mortar (thinset). Apply a layer of mortar with a wallboard knife, embed the tape into the mortar, then smooth and level the mortar.

Variation: Finishing Cementboard ▶

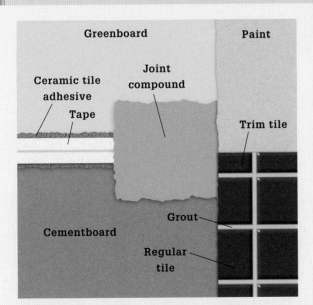

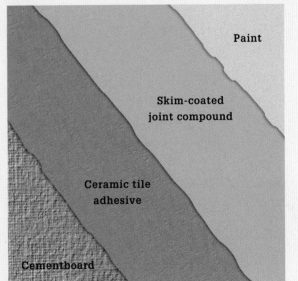

To finish a joint between cementboard and greenboard, seal the joint and exposed cementboard with ceramic tile adhesive, a mixture of four parts adhesive to one part water. Embed paper joint tape into the adhesive, smoothing the tape with a tape knife. Allow the adhesive to dry, then finish the joint with at least two coats of all-purpose wallboard joint compound.

To finish small areas of cementboard that will not be tiled, seal the cementboard with ceramic tile adhesive, a mixture of four parts adhesive to one part water, then apply a skim-coat of all-purpose wallboard joint compound, using a 12" wallboard knife. Then paint the wall.

Installing Wall Membranes

Wall membranes may provide waterproofing or isolation from small underlayment movement, or both. Because water does not sit on wall surfaces as it does on floors, waterproofing of walls is not as critical. In most cases, plastic sheeting or building paper behind cement backer board is sufficient. Saunas and steam rooms may need additional waterproofing.

Isolation membrane comes in roll- or trowel-on forms as well as in sheet form. It can be applied to existing cracks or potential areas of movement. Check the product directions for the maximum width crack or expansion joint that can be

spanned and the type of substrate on which it can be used.

It is important to apply isolation membrane to concrete walls to prevent hairline cracks from being transferred outward to the tile or grout surface. Some products combine waterproofing and isolation properties. The tile adhesive is applied directly to the isolation membrane after it has cured.

Be sure to check for compatibility between the roll- or trowel-on membranes and your particular application needs. Fountains and pools have specific waterproofing needs—check with your tile dealer if you plan on using wall tile for a pool wall.

Plastic sheeting, sheet membrane, building paper, and trowel-applied membrane are all options for adding waterproofing to walls. Isolation membranes in strips or sheets also protect tile surfaces from cracking caused by small movements in the underlayment.

A water barrier of 4-mil plastic sheeting can be stapled to studs before installing cementboard or fiber-cement board.

Building paper (15#) can also be used as a water barrier behind cementboard and fiber-cement board. Start from the bottom and install horizontally so each layer overlaps the previous one by two inches.

Waterproofing/isolation membranes are an easy way to add waterproofing and crack protection to existing walls. This application is especially suited to smooth, solid concrete surfaces. The tile adhesive is applied directly to the membrane after it dries.

Isolation membrane may be used on wall and ceiling surfaces in areas such as steam rooms and saunas that have extreme temperature fluctuation and high humidity. The membrane is typically installed with mortar, but some membranes must be used with a specific bonding agent.

Appendix: Handling Tile Materials

This chapter brings you back to basics: cutting, setting, and grouting tile. No matter how carefully you lay out an installation, chances are good that some tile will have to be cut. In large rooms with square corners and few obstructions, this will be a simple matter. In smaller rooms that have protruding pipes and objects, cutting tile accurately is one of the most important parts of the project. In the following pages, you'll find instructions on making straight cuts as well as curves, notches, and holes. You'll also find advice on choosing the right tools for the job and tips on how to use them.

Next, comes information on how to mix and use mortar. Again, this is simple but vital information. Mixing mortar is either a relatively simple process or an irritating one, depending on how you go about doing it. The information presented here helps you do it right the first time, every time.

Finally, you'll find information on grouting the finished project. It is a simple process that's made even simpler by the hints and suggestions included in these pages.

In This Chapter:

- Purchasing Materials
- Cutting Tile
- Mixing & Using Mortar

Purchasing Materials

Before you can select or purchase materials, you'll need to figure out exactly what you need and how much. Start by drawing a room layout, a reference for you and for anyone advising you about the project.

To estimate the amount of tile you need for a floor project, calculate the square footage of the room and add five percent for waste. For example, in a 10-foot × 12-foot room, the total area is 120 square feet. (12' × 10' = 120 sq. ft.). Add five percent, 6 square feet, for breakage and other waste (120 × .05 = 6 sq. ft.). You need to purchase enough tile to cover 126 square feet.

Tile cartons generally indicate the number of square feet one carton will cover. Divide the square footage to be covered by the square footage contained in a carton in order to determine the number of cartons required for your floor project. For example, if a carton holds 10 square feet, you will need 13 cartons to cover the 10 × 12 floor in our example.

Estimating tile for a wall project is slightly more complex. Start by deciding how much of each wall will be tiled. In a shower, plan to tile to at least 6" above the showerhead. It's common for tile to extend 4 feet up the remaining walls, although it's possible and sometimes very attractive for full walls to be tiled.

To calculate the amount of field tile required, measure each wall and multiply the width times the height of the area to be covered. Subtract the square footage of doors and windows. Do this for each wall, then add all the figures together to calculate the total square footage. Add five percent for waste. Calculate the number of cartons necessary (square footage of the project divided by the square footage contained in a carton).

Trim for floors and walls is sold by the lineal foot. Measure the lineal footage and calculate based on that. Plan carefully—the cost of trim tile adds up quickly. See pages 32 to 35 for further information on trim types and styles.

Before buying the tiles, ask about the dealer's return policy. Most dealers allow you to return unused tiles for a refund. In any case, think of it this way: buying a few too many tiles is a small problem. Running out of tiles when the job's almost done could turn into disaster if you can no longer get the tile or the colors don't match.

How to Purchase Materials

Use your room drawing to identify all the types of trim that will be necessary (above). Evaluate the trim available for the various tiles you're considering and select a combination that meets the specifications of your project.

Buy all necessary tile, tools, and materials at once to avoid wasted trips and to make sure all the elements are appropriate for one another and the project.

Design and paint your own custom tiles at many specialty ceramic stores. Order tile of the right size and have them bisque-fired but not glazed. You can then paint or stencil designs on the tile and have them fired. Look in the phone book for specialty ceramic stores.

Mix tile from carton to carton. Slight variations in color won't be as noticeable mixed throughout the project as they would be if the color shifts from one area to another.

Cutting Tile

Careful planning will help you eliminate unnecessary cuts, but most tile jobs require cutting at least a few tiles and some jobs require cutting a large number of tiles, no matter how carefully you plan. For a few straight cuts on light- to medium-weight tile, use a snap cutter. If you're working with heavy tile or a large number of cuts on any kind of tile, a wet saw greatly simplifies the job. When using a wet saw, wear safety glasses and hearing protection. Make sure the blade is in good condition and the water container is full. Never use the saw without water, even for a few seconds.

Other cutting tools include nippers, hand-held tile cutters, and rod saws. Nippers can be used on most types of tile, but a rod saw is most effective with wall tile, which generally is fairly soft.

A note of caution: hand-held tile cutters and tile nippers can create razor-sharp edges. Handle freshly cut tile carefully, and immediately round over the edges with a tile stone.

Before beginning a project, practice making straight and curved cuts on scrap tile.

How to Cut Tile

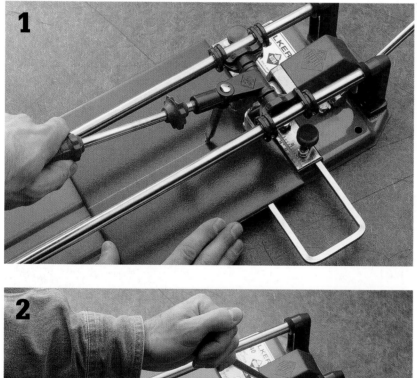

Mark a cutting line on the tile with a pencil, then place the tile in the cutter so the cutting wheel is directly over the line. While pressing down firmly on the wheel handle, run the wheel across the tile to score the surface. For a clean cut, score the tile only once.

Snap the tile along the scored line, as directed by the tool manufacturer. Usually, snapping the tile is accomplished by depressing a lever on the tile cutter.

How to Use a Wet Saw

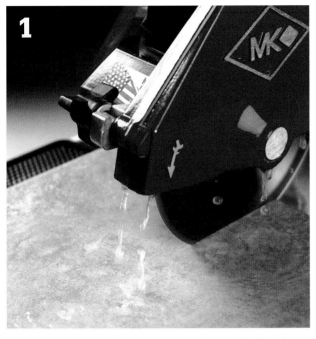

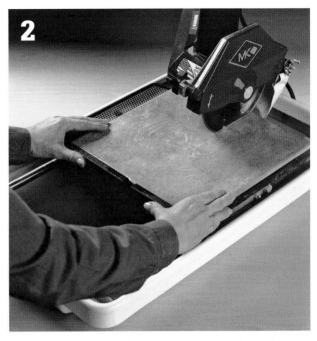

Individual saws vary, so read the manufacturer's directions for use and make sure you understand them. Refer any questions to the rental center. Wear safety glasses and hearing protection; make sure water is reaching the blade at all times.

Place the tile on the sliding table and lock the fence to hold the tile in place, then press down on the tile as you slide it past the blade.

How to Mark Square Notches

Place the tile to be notched over the last full tile on one side of the corner. Set another full tile against the ½" spacer along the wall and trace along the opposite edge onto the second tile.

Move the top two tiles and spacer to the adjoining wall, making sure not to turn the tile that is being marked. Make a second mark on the tile as in step 1. Cut the tile and install.

How to Cut Square Notches

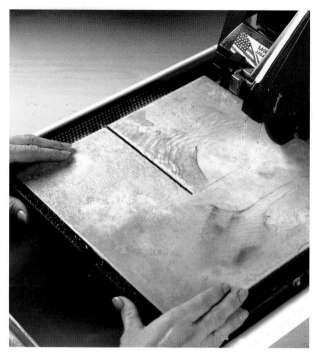

Cut along the marked line on one side of the notch. Turn the tile and cut along the other line to complete the notch. To keep the tile from breaking before you're through, slow down as you get close to the intersection with the first cut.

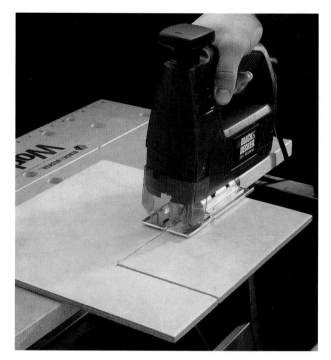

To cut square notches in a small number of wall tiles, clamp the tile down on a worktable, then use a jigsaw with a tungsten carbide blade to make the cuts. If you need to notch quite a few tiles, a wet saw is more efficient.

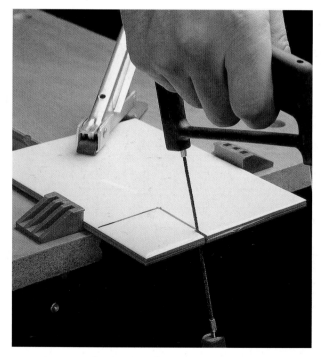

To make a small number of cuts in wall tile, you can use a rod saw. Fit a tungsten carbide rod saw into a hacksaw body. Firmly support the tile and use a sawing motion to cut the tile.

To make a very small notch, use tile nippers. Score the lines and then nibble up to the lines, biting very small pieces at a time.

How to Mark & Cut Irregular Notches

Make a paper template of the contour or use a contour gauge. To use a contour gauge, press the gauge onto the profile and trace it onto the tile.

Use a wet saw to make a series of closely spaced, parallel cuts, then nip away the waste.

How to Make Curved Cuts

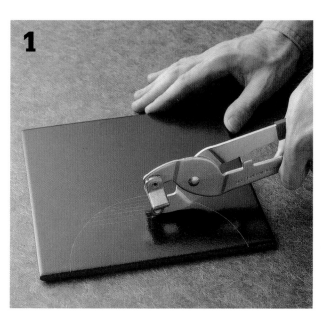

Mark a cutting line on the tile face, then use the scoring wheel of a hand-held tile cutter to score the cut line. Make several parallel scores, no more than ¼" apart, in the waste portion of the tile.

Use tile nippers to nibble away the scored portion of the tile.

How to Mark & Cut Holes in Tile

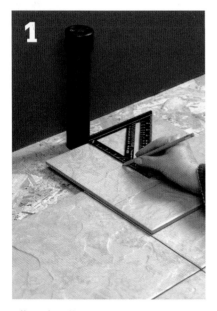

Align the tile to be cut with the last full row of tile and butt it against the pipe. Mark the center of the pipe onto the front edge of the tile.

Place a ¼" spacer against the wall and butt the tile against it. Mark the pipe center on the side edge of the tile. Using a combination square, draw a line through each mark to the edges of the tile.

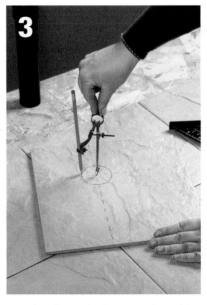

Starting from the intersection of the lines at the center, draw a circle slightly larger than the pipe or protrusion.

Drill around the edges of the hole, using a ceramic tile bit. Gently knock out the waste material with a hammer. The rough edges of the hole will be covered by a protective plate (called an escutcheon).

Variation: Score and cut the tile so the hole is divided in half, using the straight-cut method (page 254), then use the curved-cut method (page 257) to remove waste material from each half of the circle.

How to Drill Holes in Tile

1

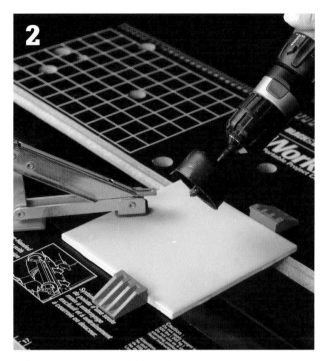

2

Make a dimple with a center punch to break through the glaze, to keep the drill bit from wandering.

Select a tungsten carbide hole saw in the appropriate size and attach it to a power drill. Place the tip at the marked center and drill the hole.

Making Specialty Cuts ▸

Score cuts on mosaic tiles with a tile cutter in the row where the cut will occur. Cut away excess strips of mosaics from the sheet, using a utility knife, then use a handheld tile cutter to snap tiles one at a time. *Note: Use tile nippers to cut narrow portions of tiles after scoring.*

Mixing & Using Mortar

Thinset mortar is a fine-grained cement product used to adhere underlayment to the subfloor and to bond ceramic tile to underlayment. Some mortars include a latex additive in the dry mix, but with others, you'll need to add liquid latex additive as you prepare the mortar.

When mixing mortar, start with the dry powder and gradually add water, stirring the mixture to achieve a creamy consistency. You want the mortar wet enough for the tiles to stick, but not so wet that it's runny. Once the mortar is spread on the floor or wall, the ridges of the mortar should hold their shape.

Mortar is spread on the underlayment or substrate with a notched trowel. The edge of the trowel creates furrows in the mortar bed, then tile is placed on the mortar using a twisting motion.

As you install tiles, spread only as much mortar as you can use in 10 minutes. If the mortar sits too long, it will begin to harden and the tiles will not adhere to it. If it does begin to harden, scrape it up, throw it away, and spread new mortar.

How to Mix Mortar

To prepare small batches (above), add liquid, a little at a time, to the dry powder and stir the mixture until it has a creamy consistency. If you're adding liquid latex additive, mix it in when the mixture nears the proper consistency.

To prepare large batches or a series of batches (above), use a ½" drill and a mortar mixing paddle. This job easily can burn out a standard ⅜" drill, so it's worth the money to rent a heavy-duty drill if you don't have one.

Options for Mortaring Tile

Spread mortar evenly onto the floor, using the appropriate trowel. Use the notched edge of the trowel to create furrows in the mortar bed.

Butter individual tiles by applying thinset mortar directly to the back of the tile. Use the notched edge of the trowel to furrow the mortar.

Butter each wall tile and apply it to the wall with a slight twisting motion.

Variation: Spread the mortar on a small section of wall, then set the tiles into it. Thinset mortar sets quickly, so work quickly if you choose this method.

Glossary

American National Standards Institute (ANSI): A standards-making organization that rates tile for water permeability.

Art tiles: Hand-finished tiles with designs, pictures, or patterns. Art tiles are often used to accent a large tile layout.

Back buttering: Spreading mortar on the back of a tile before pressing it onto the substrate.

Baseboard tile: Baseboard-shaped tiles used to replace wood baseboards.

Bullnose trim tile: Tile with one rounded edge that is meant to be left exposed.

Cement body tile: Tile made from concrete poured into forms.

Coefficient of friction: The measure of a tile's slip resistance. Tiles with high numbers are more slip-resistant.

Decorative: Tile with designs, pictures, or relief. Decorative tiles are generally used as accents in a field of solid-color tiles.

Dry fit: Installing tile without mortar in order to test the layout.

Expansion joint: An expansion joint is a joint in a tile layout filled with a flexible material like caulk instead of grout. The expansion joint allows the tile to shift without cracking.

Field tiles: The main tile in a tile design. As opposed to trim or accent tiles.

Floor tile: Any type of tile designated for use on floors. It can generally also be used for walls or countertops.

Floor-warming systems: A system of heating elements installed directly under the floor material. Floor-warming systems are intended to provide supplemental radiant heat for a room.

Glass tile: Tile made of translucent glass. Glass tile is often used as accent tile.

Glazed ceramic: Tile made from refined clay that has been coated with a glaze and then fired in a kiln.

Grade: Ratings applied to some tile indicating the quality and consistency of manufacturing. Grade 1 tile is standard, suitable for most applications; grade 2 may have minor glaze and size imperfections; grade 3 tile is thin and suitable only for wall or decorative applications.

Grout: A dry powder, usually cement based, that is mixed with water and pressed into the joints between tiles. Grout also comes with latex or acrylic added for greater adhesion and impermeability.

Impervious: Tile that absorbs less than .5% of its weight in water.

Isolation membrane: Isolation membrane is a flexible material installed in sheets or troweled onto an unstable or damaged base floor, subfloor, or wall before installing tile. The isolation membrane prevents shifts in the base from damaging the tile above.

Joists: The framing members that support the floor.

Kiln: A high-temperature oven used to harden clay tile.

Liners: Narrow tiles used for adding contrasting lines to tile layouts.

Listello: A border tile, usually with a raised design. Also called listel.

Mastic or organic mastic: A type of glue for installing tile. It comes premixed and cures as it dries. It is convenient for wall tiles smaller than 6 × 6, but it is not suitable for floors.

Metal tile: Tile made of iron, stainless steel, copper, or brass. Metal tile is often used as accent tile.

Mortar or thinset mortar: A mixture of portland cement and sand and occasionally a latex or acrylic additive to improve adhesion.

Mosaic tile: Small colored tiles used to make patterns or pictures on walls and floors.

Natural stone tile: Tile cut from marble, slate, granite, or other natural stone.

Non-vitreous: Very permeable tile. Non-vitreous tile absorbs more than 7% of its total weight in water. Not suitable for outdoor installations.

Porcelain Enamel Institute (PEI): A tile industry group that issues ratings on tile's resistance to wear.

Porcelain tile: Tile made from refined white clay fired at high temperatures. Porcelain is usually dyed rather than glazed, and thus its color runs the tile's full thickness.

Quarry tile: Tile formed to look like quarried stone.

Reference lines: Lines marked on the substrate to guide the placement of the first row of tile.

Saltillo: Terra-cotta tile from Mexico. Saltillos have a distinctly rustic appearance.

Sealants: Sealants protect non- and semi-vitreous tile from stains and from water damage. Sealants are also important for protecting grout.

Self-spacing tile: Tile with attached tabs for maintaining even spacing.

Semi-vitreous: Moderately permeable tile. Absorbs 3-7% of its total weight in water. Not suitable for outdoor installations.

Spacers: Plastic lugs meant to be inserted between tiles to help maintain uniform spacing during installation.

Story stick: A length of 1×2 lumbar marked with the tile spacing for a specific layout.

Subfloor: The surface, usually made of plywood, attached to the floor joists.

Substrates or underlayment: A surface installed on top of an existing floor, subfloor, or wall. The substrate creates a suitable surface for installing tile. Substrate materials include cementboard, plywood, cork, backerboard, greenboard, or water-proofing membrane.

Terra-cotta tile: Tile made from unrefined clay. Terra-cotta is fired at low temperature. Its color varies greatly depending on where the source of the clay.

Trim tile: Tile with a finished edge for completing wall tile layouts.

V-cap tiles: V- or L-shaped tile for finishing the exposed edges of countertops.

Vitreous: Slightly permeable tile. Absorbs .5-3% of its total weight in water.

Wall tile: Tile intended for use on walls. It is generally thinner than floor tile and should not be used on floors or countertops.

Water absorption or permeability: The measure of the amount of water that will penetrate a tile when it is wet. Measurement ranges from non-vitreous to semi-vitreous to vitreous to impervious.

Waterproofing membrane: A flexible, water-proof material installed in sheets or brushed on to protect the subfloor from water damage.

Resources

American Society of Interior Designers
202-546-3480
www.asid.org

Center for Universal Design NC State University
919-515-3082
www.design.ncsu.edu/cud

Ceramic Tiles of Italy
www.italiatiles.com

Clay Squared to Infinity
612-781-6409
www.claysquared.com

Construction Materials Recycling Association
630-548-4510
www.cdrecycling.org

Cool Tiles
1-888-TILES-88 (888-845-3788)
www.cooltiles.com

Crossville Porcelain Stone
931-484-2110
www.crossvilleceramics.com

Daltile
800-933-TILE

d'facto Art, Inc.
952-906-1003
www.dfactoart.com

Energy & Environmental Building Association
952-881-1098
www.eeba.org

EuroTile Featuring Villi®Glas
239-275-8033
www.villiglass.com

Fireclay Tile, Inc.
408-275-1182
www.fireclaytile.com

Hakatai Enterprises, Inc.
888-667-2429
www.hakatai.com

Hi-Ho Industries, Inc.
Mosaic-Tile Arts
651-649-0992

IKEA Home Furnishings
610-834-0180
www.Ikea-USA.com

International Residential Code Book
International Conference of Building Officials
800-284-4406
www.icbo.com

KPTiles
Kristen Phillips
248-853-0418
www.kptiles.com

Meredith Collection
330-484-4887
www.meredithtile.com

Montana Tile & Stone Co.
406-587-6114
www.montanatile.com

National Kitchen & Bath Association (NKBA)
800-843-6522
www.nkba.org

Oceanside Glasstile™
760-929-5882
www.glasstile.com

The Tile Shop
800.433.2939
www.tileshop.com

Tile Creator™
760-788-1288
www.tilecreator.com

Walker & Zanger, Inc.
818-504-0235
www.walkersanger.com

Rubble Tile
952-938-2599
www.rubbletile.com

US Environmental Protection Agency, Indoor Air Quality
www.epa.gov/iedweb00/pubs/insidest.html

Photographers

Courtesy of 18 Montana & Stone Co.
p. 52 (top left), 90 (top)

Baerdemaeker / Inside / Beateworks.com
p. 146 (top)

Brian Vanden Brink
p. 20, 28, 157 (left)

Courtesy of Buddy Rhodes Studio
p. 52 (lower)

Courtesy of Ceramic Tiles of Italy
p. 4, 6 (lower left), 8 (left), 8 (right), 10, 13 (right), 17
(lower), 22, 23, 24 (top and lower), 25 (top), 27, 29
(lower), 30 (left and right), 31, 45, 50, 52 (top right), 53
(lower), 54 (lower left), 79 (middle), 80, 87 (top, middle,
lower), 88, 90 (lower right), 91, 92 (top and lower),
93 (lower), 94, 95 (top and lower), 96, 127 (top left),
129 (lower), 146 (lower), 147 (top left and right), 147
(lower), 148 (lower right), 150 (lower), 151 (top), 170,
175, 177 (top)

Claessens / Inside / Beateworks.com
p. 93 (top right)

Crossville Porcelain Stone
p. 6 (top), 6 (lower right), 7, 13 (left), 15 (left), 43 (top), 54
(top right), 126, 127 (top right), 127 (lower right), 173
(lower), 174 (lower), 177 (lower)

Courtesy of Daltile
p. 16, 17 (top), 106 (top)

Duronsoy / Inside / Beateworks.com
p. 172 (top)

Eric Roth
p. 19, 21 (top), 26 (top), 29 (top), 31

Courtesy of Fireclay Tile, Inc.
p. 157 (right)

FotoKia / Index Stock Imagery Inc.
p. 177 (lower)

Courtesy of Hakatai Enterprises, Inc.
p. 9 (left), 9 (right), 18 (top), 124, 129 (top), 144

Henry Cabala / Beateworks.com
p. 149

Courtesy of Ikea Home Furnishings
p. 26 (lower), 54 (lower right)

Jessie Walker
p. 21 (lower), 25 (lower)

Courtesy of National Kitchen & Bath Association
p. 18 (lower)

Courtesy of Oceanside Glasstile™
p. 15 (right) / Christopher Ray Photography

Shubroto Chattopadhyay / Index Stock Imagery Inc.
p. 176 (lower)

Stephen Saks / Index Stock Imagery Inc.
p. 176 (top)

Tim Street-Porter
p. 38, 90 (lower left), 93 (top left), 127 (lower left), 128,
150 (top), 172 (lower), 173 (top), 174 (top)

Van Robaeys / Inside / Beateworks.com
p. 53 (top)

Vasseur / Inside / Beateworks.com
p. 55

Courtesy of Walker Zanger, Inc.
p. 54 (top left)

Conversion Charts

Lumber Dimensions

Nominal - U.S.	Actual - U.S. (in inches)	Metric
1 × 2	¾ × 1½	19 × 38 mm
1 × 3	¾ × 2½	19 × 64 mm
1 × 4	¾ × 3½	19 × 89 mm
1 × 5	¾ × 4½	19 × 114 mm
1 × 6	¾ × 5½	19 × 140 mm
1 × 7	¾ × 6¼	19 × 159 mm
1 × 8	¾ × 7¼	19 × 184 mm
1 × 10	¾ × 9¼	19 × 235 mm
1 × 12	¾ × 11¼	19 × 286 mm
1¼ × 4	1 × 3½	25 × 89 mm
1¼ × 6	1 × 5½	25 × 140 mm
1¼ × 8	1 × 7¼	25 × 184 mm
1¼ × 10	1 × 9¼	25 × 235 mm
1¼ × 12	1 × 11¼	25 × 286 mm

Nominal - U.S.	Actual - U.S. (in inches)	Metric
1½ × 4	1¼ × 3½	32 × 89 mm
1½ × 6	1¼ × 5½	32 × 140 mm
1½ × 8	1¼ × 7¼	32 × 184 mm
1½ × 10	1¼ × 9¼	32 × 235 mm
1½ × 12	1¼ × 11¼	32 × 286 mm
2 × 4	1½ × 3½	38 × 89 mm
2 × 6	1½ × 5½	38 × 140 mm
2 × 8	1½ × 7¼	38 × 184 mm
2 × 10	1½ × 9¼	38 × 235 mm
2 × 12	1½ × 11¼	38 × 286 mm
3 × 6	2½ × 5½	64 × 140 mm
4 × 4	3½ × 3½	89 × 89 mm
4 × 6	3½ × 5½	89 × 140 mm

Metric Conversions

To Convert:	To:	Multiply by:
Inches	Millimeters	25.4
Inches	Centimeters	25.4
Feet	Meters	0.305
Yards	Meters	0.914
Square inches	Square centimeters	6.45
Square feet	Square meters	0.093
Square yards	Square meters	0.836
Ounces	Milliliters	30.0
Pints (U.S.)	Liters	0.473 (Imp. 0.568)
Quarts (U.S.)	Liters	0.946 (Imp. 1.136)
Gallons (U.S.)	Liters	3.785 (Imp. 4.546)
Ounces	Grams	28.4
Pounds	Kilograms	0.454

To Convert:	To:	Multiply by:
Millimeters	Inches	0.039
Centimeters	Inches	0.394
Meters	Feet	3.28
Meters	Yards	1.09
Square centimeters	Square inches	0.155
Square meters	Square feet	10.8
Square meters	Square yards	1.2
Milliliters	Ounces	.033
Liters	Pints (U.S.)	2.114 (Imp. 1.76)
Liters	Quarts (U.S.)	1.057 (Imp. 0.88)
Liters	Gallons (U.S.)	0.264 (Imp. 0.22)
Grams	Ounces	0.035
Kilograms	Pounds	2.2

Counterbore, Shank & Pilot Hole Diameters

Screw Size	Counterbore Diameter for Screw Head (in inches)	Clearance Hole for Screw Shank (in inches)	Pilot Hole Diameter Hard Wood (in inches)	Soft Wood (in inches)
#1	.146 (⁹⁄₆₄)	⁵⁄₆₄	³⁄₆₄	¹⁄₃₂
#2	¼	³⁄₃₂	³⁄₆₄	¹⁄₃₂
#3	¼	⁷⁄₆₄	¹⁄₁₆	³⁄₆₄
#4	¼	⅛	¹⁄₁₆	³⁄₆₄
#5	¼	⅛	⁵⁄₆₄	¹⁄₁₆
#6	⁵⁄₁₆	⁹⁄₆₄	³⁄₃₂	⁵⁄₆₄
#7	⁵⁄₁₆	⁵⁄₃₂	³⁄₃₂	⁵⁄₆₄
#8	⅜	¹¹⁄₆₄	⅛	³⁄₃₂
#9	⅜	¹¹⁄₆₄	⅛	³⁄₃₂
#10	⅜	³⁄₁₆	⅛	⁷⁄₆₄
#11	½	³⁄₁₆	⁵⁄₃₂	⁹⁄₆₄
#12	½	⁷⁄₃₂	⁹⁄₆₄	⅛

Saw Blades

Carbide blade   Panel blade   Planer blade   Masonry blade   Metal-cutting blade

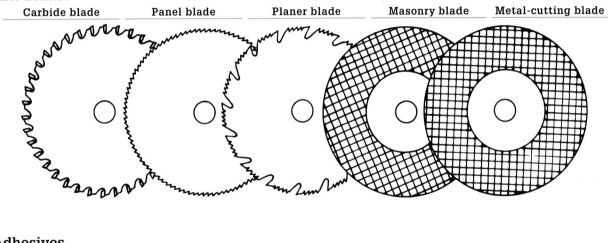

Adhesives

Type	Characteristics	Uses
White glue	**Strength:** moderate; rigid bond **Drying time:** several hours **Resistance to heat:** poor **Resistance to moisture:** poor **Hazards:** none **Cleanup/solvent:** soap and water	**Porous surfaces:** Wood (indoors) Paper Cloth
Yellow glue (carpenter's glue)	**Strength:** moderate to good; rigid bond **Drying time:** several hours; faster than white glue **Resistance to heat:** moderate **Resistance to moisture:** moderate **Hazards:** none **Cleanup/solvent:** soap and water	**Porous surfaces:** Wood (indoors) Paper Cloth
Two-part epoxy	**Strength:** excellent; strongest of all adhesives **Drying time:** varies, depending on manufacturer **Resistance to heat:** excellent **Resistance to moisture:** excellent **Hazards:** fumes are toxic and flammable **Cleanup/solvent:** acetone will dissolve some types	**Smooth & porous surfaces:** Wood (indoors & outdoors) Metal Masonry Glass Fiberglass
Hot glue	**Strength:** depends on type **Drying time:** less than 60 seconds **Resistance to heat:** fair **Resistance to moisture:** good **Hazards:** hot glue can cause burns **Cleanup/solvent:** heat will loosen bond	**Smooth & porous surfaces:** Glass Plastics Wood
Cyanoacrylate (instant glue)	**Strength:** excellent, but with little flexibility **Drying time:** a few seconds **Resistance to heat:** excellent **Resistance to moisture:** excellent **Hazards:** can bond skin instantly; toxic, flammable **Cleanup/solvent:** acetone	**Smooth surfaces:** Glass Ceramics Plastics Metal
Construction adhesive	**Strength:** good to excellent; very durable **Drying time:** 24 hours **Resistance to heat:** good **Resistance to moisture:** excellent **Hazards:** may irritate skin and eyes **Cleanup/solvent:** soap and water (while still wet)	**Porous surfaces:** Framing lumber Plywood and paneling Wallboard Foam panels Masonry
Water-base contact cement	**Strength:** good **Drying time:** bonds instantly; dries fully in 30 minutes **Resistance to heat:** excellent **Resistance to moisture:** good **Hazards:** may irritate skin and eyes **Cleanup/solvent:** soap and water (while still wet)	**Porous surfaces:** Plastic laminates Plywood Flooring Cloth
Silicone sealant (caulk)	**Strength:** fair to good; very flexible bond **Drying time:** 24 hours **Resistance to heat:** good **Resistance to moisture:** excellent **Hazards:** may irritate skin and eyes **Cleanup/solvent:** acetone	**Smooth & porous surfaces:** Wood Ceramics Fiberglass Plastics Glass

Index

Also From **CREATIVE PUBLISHING** international

Complete Guide to Attics & Basements

Complete Guide to Bathrooms

Complete Guide Build Your Kids a Treehouse

Complete Guide to Ceramic & Stone Tile

Complete Guide to Creative Landscapes

Complete Guide to Custom Shelves & Built-Ins

Complete Guide to Decks

Complete Guide to Dream Kitchens

Complete Guide to Easy Woodworking Projects

Complete Guide to Finishing Walls & Ceilings

Complete Guide to Floor Décor

Complete Guide to Gazebos & Arbors

Complete Guide to Home Carpentry

Complete Guide to Home Plumbing

Complete Guide to Home Wiring

Complete Guide to Landscape Construction

Complete Guide Maintain Your Pool & Spa

Complete Guide to Masonry & Stonework

Complete Guide to Outdoor Wood Projects

Complete Guide to Painting & Decorating

Complete Guide to Patios

Complete Guide to Roofing & Siding

Complete Guide to Trim & Finish Carpentry

Complete Guide to Windows & Doors

Complete Guide to Wood Storage Projects

Complete Guide to Yard & Garden Features

Complete Outdoor Builder

Complete Photo Guide to Home Repair

Complete Photo Guide to Home Improvement

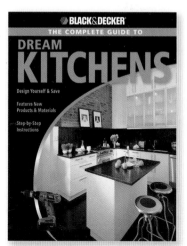

ISBN 1-58923-304-2

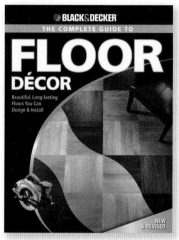

ISBN 1-58923-332-8

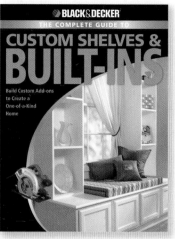

ISBN 1-58923-303-4

Creative Publishing
international

18705 Lake Drive East • Chanhassen, MN 55317 • www.creativepub.com